TRUE DETECTIVE AND PHILOSOPHY

The Blackwell Philosophy and Pop Culture Series
Series editor William Irwin

A spoonful of sugar helps the medicine go down, and a healthy helping of popular culture clears the cobwebs from Kant. Philosophy has had a public relations problem for a few centuries now. This series aims to change that, showing that philosophy is relevant to your life—and not just for answering the big questions like "To be or not to be?" but for answering the little questions: "To watch or not to watch *South Park?*" Thinking deeply about TV, movies, and music doesn't make you a "complete idiot." In fact it might make you a philosopher, someone who believes the unexamined life is not worth living and the unexamined cartoon is not worth watching.

Already published in the series:

TRUE DETECTIVE AND PHILOSOPHY

A DEEPER KIND OF DARKNESS

Edited by

Jacob Graham and Tom Sparrow

WILEY Blackwell

Registered Offices
John Wiley & Sons, Inc., 111 River Street, Hoboken, NJ 07030, USA
John Wiley & Sons Ltd, The Atrium, Southern Gate, Chichester, West Sussex, PO19 8SQ, UK

Editorial Office
9600 Garsington Road, Oxford, OX4 2DQ, UK

For details of our global editorial offices, customer services, and more information about Wiley products visit us at www.wiley.com.

Wiley also publishes its books in a variety of electronic formats and by print-on-demand. Some content that appears in standard print versions of this book may not be available in other formats.

Library of Congress Cataloging-in-Publication Data

Names: Graham, Jacob editor. | Sparrow, Tom, 1979– editor.
Title: True detective and philosophy : a deeper kind of darkness / edited by Jacob Graham, Tom Sparrow.
Description: Hoboken : Wiley, 2018. | Series: The Blackwell philosophy and popculture series | Includes bibliographical references and index. | Identifiers: LCCN 2017014278 (print) | LCCN 2017028324 (ebook) | ISBN 9781119280798 (pdf) | ISBN 9781119280828 (epub) | ISBN 9781119280781 (pbk.)
Subjects: LCSH: True detective (Television program)
Classification: LCC PN1992.77.T79 (ebook) | LCC PN1992.77.T79 T78 2017 (print) | DDC 791.45/72–dc23
LC record available at https://lccn.loc.gov/2017014278

Cover Design: Wiley
Cover Images: Guy © 4x6/Gettyimages; Texture © TothGaborGyula/Gettyimages; Forest © odebala/Gettyimages

Set in 11/13pt SabonLTStd by Aptara Inc., New Delhi, India

10 9 8 7 6 5 4 3 2 1

Contents

Introduction
Welcome to the Psychosphere

Jacob Graham and Tom Sparrow

If you're anything like us, you enjoy listening to Rust wax philosophical as much as you like watching Marty balk at the odd shit
that comes out of Rust's mouth. When it comes to big questions
about value, meaning, truth, and existence, these characters
couldn't be further apart. Professionally, on the other hand, they
complement each other pretty well: they get the job done, solve the
case. For two guys responsible for enforcing the law, however, their
moral compasses don't always point them in the right direction.
Which is not to say that the officers in Vinci shoot any straighter.
Remember that time Velcoro kicked the crap out of Aspen Con-
roy's father right in front of the kid? Of course you do. It was kind
of wrong, but felt kind of right, didn't it? The cops in *True Detective* can be as twisted as the backroads of the Louisiana bayou
and the freeways of Los Angeles. They're defined as much by their
deceit, disloyalty, substance abuse, self-loathing, and violence as
they are their compassion, duty, and peculiar sense of justice.

As we ride along with Cohle and Hart or Bezzerides and
Velcoro, it's impossible not to marvel at the bleak Louisiana and
California landscapes. Drenched in shadow, foretelling something
sinister, they are populated by masked men, cruel and murderous—
the worst kinds of men. Corruption, decay, and degradation touch
everything. And yet, we viewers choose to linger in those desolate
landscapes, happily pursuing real-life monsters in the squad car of
our true detectives, enthralled by the promise of some unforeseen
horror. But why do we watch? What draws us in? Do we detect

something of ourselves in these worlds? That should worry us. Do we know who we really are? There'd be a victory in that.

We'll leave it for you to decide where you fit in the picture or what makes for a true detective, but we'd like to suggest that detectives and philosophers have something in common—both seek the truth—and that *True Detective* can teach us a lot about philosophy. Unlike detective work, however, and fortunately for us, the risk of imminent physical harm is low with philosophy. Yet, the stakes are still high, especially if, as Socrates (470–399 BCE) said, "the unexamined life is not worth living." Through the eyes of the characters and the stories of *True Detective*, the squad of authors in this book pull back the curtain on some philosophical ideas more powerful than any cultic demigod or corrupt mayor. By exposing the philosophical roots and contexts of pessimism, our squad uncovers just why Rust is so bad at parties. Examining topics such as good and evil, tragedy, personal identity, and time, they introduce us to philosophers such as Socrates, Schopenhauer, Nietzsche, Lacan, and Žižek. Ultimately, though, you must become your own detective and figure out the truth for yourself.

So, why should you, dear reader, continue beyond this introduction? Because you have a debt. You owe it to yourself to do some truth detecting, to step back into the forsaken world of *True Detective* where ominous shadows grow ever darker and stories are told with facts and lies. We're not asking you to make this journey one of silent reflection. We want you to figure out for yourself what you think, to give yourself the philosophical world that you deserve, and to remove the mask from the truth that lives among us, well disguised.

Part I

"IT'S ALL ONE GHETTO, MAN ... A GIANT GUTTER IN OUTER SPACE"

Pessimism and Anti-natalism

Why Life Rather than Death?
Answers from Rustin Cohle and Arthur Schopenhauer[1]

Sandra Shapshay

Rustin Cohle, the protagonist of the first season of *True Detective*, declares that he is "in philosophical terms, a pessimist." Before we are introduced to him, Rust has already experienced the terrible loss of his two-year-old daughter and the painful dissolution of his marriage. His employment confronts him daily with the horrors of human conduct, where the "law of the stronger" reigns and the strong and sadistic exploit the weak and vulnerable. Throughout season one, we see Rust struggling to find the best, truest response to all this seemingly endemic and unredeemed suffering.

Rust thinks that human consciousness is a "tragic misstep in nature." The doctrine of "pessimism" espoused by Rust is remarkably similar to the view adumbrated by Arthur Schopenhauer (1788–1860), who holds that (1) conscious life (both human and nonhuman animal) involves a tremendous amount of suffering that is essentially *built into the structure of the world* and (2) there is no Creator (providential or otherwise) to redeem all of this suffering, by, say, punishing the wicked and rewarding the good.

Arthur Schopenhauer's Pessimism

Schopenhauer is just as attuned as Rust to the tremendous amount of evil in the world, caused for the most part by other human

True Detective and Philosophy: A Deeper Kind of Darkness, First Edition.
Edited by Jacob Graham and Tom Sparrow.
© 2018 John Wiley & Sons Ltd. Published 2018 by John Wiley & Sons Ltd.

beings. Whereas the "true detective" is nauseated and jaded by the sadistic acts of bayou killers who prey mostly on innocent girls and young women, Schopenhauer is nauseated and jaded by more institutional sources of human suffering in nineteenth-century Europe and the United States that spring largely from pervasive human egoism and, to a lesser but not insignificant extent, malice:

> The chief source of the most serious evils affecting man is man himself; *homo homini lupus*. He who keeps this last fact clearly in view beholds the world as a hell, surpassing that of Dante by the fact that one man must be the devil of another. ... How man deals with man is seen, for example, in Negro slavery, the ultimate object of which is sugar and coffee. However, we need not go so far; to enter at the age of five a cotton-spinning or other factory, and from then on to sit there every day first ten, then twelve and finally fourteen hours, and perform the same mechanical work, is to purchase dearly the pleasure of drawing breath. But this is the fate of millions, and many more millions have an analogous fate.[2]

Additionally, Schopenhauer focuses on the suffering of nonhuman animals at the hands of human beings who view them as mere instruments for their use:

> Because ... Christian morals give no consideration to animals, they are at once free as birds in philosophical morals too, they are mere "things", mere *means* to whatever ends you like, as for instance vivisection, hunting with hounds, bull-fighting, racing, whipping to death in front of an immovable stone-cart and the like.[3]

Why Not Suicide?

Given this grim view of the human condition, it makes sense to raise the question of suicide: Why not put an end to one's life, in order to escape from this ultimately senseless vale of tears? Throughout *True Detective*, Rust struggles with "letting go" and, regarding the last episode of season one, "Form and Void," the creator, Nic Pizzolatto, explains that the episode "represents the dilemma Rust walked for some time: why life rather than the opposite?"[4] Rust thinks that our "programming" (in Schopenhauer's terms, the "will-to-live") "gets us out of bed in the morning" but that it would be better, all things considered, to "deny our programming" and walk ourselves "hand in hand into extinction" ("The Long Bright Dark"). Thus, Rust enunciates his *in principle* embrace of suicide.

In this positive attitude toward suicide, Rust actually parts ways with Schopenhauer, which is surprising since the philosopher is one of the most famous pessimists in the history of Western thought. In fact, Schopenhauer regarded suicide as a "futile and foolish act."[5] What accounts for this divergence?

Schopenhauer's Answer

Schopenhauer does not discourage suicide out of philosophical optimism: he doesn't think that this is the best of all possible worlds, as Gottfried Leibniz (1646–1716) does; neither does he believe that the world *must* get better because of a necessary rational structure, as Georg Wilhelm Friedrich Hegel (1770–1831) holds; nor that the world is a self-justifying divine cause, as Baruch Spinoza (1632–1677) argues. Also, he doesn't see life as a gift, to be thankfully accepted. Schopenhauer is convinced that the world is and will always be full of unredeemed suffering, for nature involves an internecine struggle for existence rather than a "peaceable king-dom" of animals living largely in harmony. And he is convinced that much of this suffering will go uncompensated in this life, as the sources of suffering seem to outweigh the sources of happiness and tranquility. Above all, he is an uncompromising atheist who holds that there is no providential God to redeem all of this suffer-ing in an afterlife.

It might be surprising, then, that Schopenhauer thinks suicide is a "futile and foolish act." Perhaps, like Rust, Schopenhauer should embrace suicide. For the nature of the will-to-live is ultimately blind, senseless striving and suffering for no particular end. Yet the reason Schopenhauer rejects suicide is that suicide does not negate but rather affirms the will-to-live, for the person who would die by suicide *desires life*; it's just that the individual is unsatisfied with the conditions on offer for their particular life. Within this logic, suicide is foolish because it prevents a person from attaining the highest wisdom and the true inner peace that would come from actual *renunciation* of the will-to-live. Thus, Schopenhauer writes, suicide is "an act of will" through which "the individual will abolishes the body ... before suffering can break it." He thereby likens a suicidal person to a sick person who "having started undergoing a painful operation that could cure him completely, does not allow it to be completed and would rather stay sick."[6] There is only one remarkable exception to his overall view on suicide: death by voluntary starvation. At the highest levels of asceticism, the negation of the will-to-live can attain such a point where "even the will needed to maintain the vegetative functions of the body through nutrition can fall away."[7]

Rust's Answer

Returning to *True Detective*, we see that Rust struggles with many of the same issues that occupy Schopenhauer. For instance, though Rust embraces pessimism and resignationist tendencies, as evidenced by his rather ascetic lifestyle and *in principle* embrace of suicide, Rust does not actually resign himself from life. He is, after all, the eponymous "true detective" and throws himself assiduously into the task of solving the ritualistic rapes and murders and bringing the perpetrators to justice.

So what really motivates Rust to spend most of his waking life (and he doesn't seem to sleep all that much) attempting to solve these crimes? Is it the intellectual puzzle? Is it compassion for the victims and potential new victims? Is it a thirst for justice?

At times it seems that it is merely the intellectual challenge that motivates Rust. This recalls Schopenhauer's own expressed reason to devote himself to philosophy: "Life is an unpleasant business; I have resolved to spend it reflecting upon it."[8] Yet, what preoccupies Rust's mind and takes up a good bit of wall space in his barely furnished apartment is reflection with a *specific practical aim*—namely, to solve the crimes in order to prevent future victims and to bring the perpetrators to justice.

Thus, Rust seems not just motivated by the intellectual puzzle but also by a morality of compassion and justice. After all, his aim is not merely to solve the crimes but also to apprehend or otherwise stop the perpetrators. Further, these moral motives get to the heart of Rust's espousal of pessimism in the first place, for he is—unlike how Marty often seems—acutely sensitive to the sufferings of others and—again, unlike Marty but in line with Schopenhauer—rejects any theological story of redemption for all of this suffering.

What I want to suggest, then, is that Rust's own practice belies his stated pessimistic views. It is not just "programming"—the will-to-live, egoistic striving—that gets Rust out of bed in the morning; rather, it is the sense that if there is to be any kind of redemption it has to be earthly, in the form of prevention or alleviation of suffering, and in bringing criminals to justice.

Schopenhauer on Compassion

Surprisingly, Schopenhauer at certain points in his writings seems to recommend the general, compassionate, and justice-seeking path that Rust takes in *True Detective*. Especially in his underappreciated essay "On the Basis of Morality," Schopenhauer recommends acts of justice and loving-kindness in response to the myriad sources of misery. For example, he praises the British nation's spending "up to 20 million pounds" to buy the freedom of slaves in America.[9] He also champions the proliferation of animal protection societies in Continental Europe, recommending English newspaper reports to address "the associations against the torture of animals now established in Germany, so that they see how one must attack the issue if anything is to come of it" and he acknowledges "the praiseworthy zeal of Councillor Perner in Munich who has devoted himself entirely to this branch of beneficence and spread the initiative for it throughout the whole of Germany."[10]

Finally, Schopenhauer recognizes that the work of civic organizations, especially in securing legal change, can bring about real moral change and reduce suffering. Again, with respect to the animal protection movement and laws against animal cruelty, Schopenhauer writes, "Everything adduced here gives evidence that the moral chord in question ... is gradually beginning to sound in the occidental world."[11]

Schopenhauer opposes all forms of suicide, except the redeeming ascetic one, because suicide robs a person of the highest wisdom regarding the apparent futility of life. However, the hopeful ethics of compassion that Schopenhauer also espouses looks like a second-rate option. On the traditional reading of Schopenhauer, he holds that it is better to go beyond willing and therefore beyond compassion as well to a real renunciation of the will-to-live, if one can. Only in renunciation is the patient truly cured of the rather absurd scourge that is the will-to-live. Yet, the rationality of the choice between compassionate action, on the one hand (action that tries *to improve the world*), and resignation, on the other (*inaction that constitutes a redemption from the world*), hinges on whether there are good grounds for hope.

Rust's Doubt

Returning to *True Detective*, we see Rust doubt whether there *are* good grounds for hope. The task of preventing and alleviating suffering as well as bringing a measure of justice into the world is onerous. It also threatens to seem futile given the large numbers of murders and disappearances, and the rampant cruelty and degradation inflicted especially upon children, teenage girls, and women throughout the series. This sense of futility, it seems, overtakes Rust in the interim between "solving" the first crime introduced in the show and the second spate of similar murders.

During this hiatus, Rust has indeed opted for resignation as a response to pessimism. Although he does not have the constitution for outright suicide—as he says to Marty—he is nonetheless doing a pretty good job of drinking himself to death. He has essentially retreated from the world into a dark bar where he can engage in almost nonstop anesthetization through the bottle, until a spate of new, similar murders awakens him from his resignationist slumber, resparking his intellectual curiosity as well as his compassion and sense of justice.

But it takes the final, spooky, and frankly nauseating confrontation with evil incarnate, in the form of the "Yellow King," to show Rust a *legitimate* path to the affirmation of life, as opposed to what he sees as an intellectually dishonest, optimistic, theological route. After surviving the bizarre melee and shutting down the activities of this serial killer, Rust gains a sense that perhaps his thoroughgoing pessimism is, at bottom, unwarranted. Despite the fact of tremendous suffering and injustice in the world, there are, nonetheless, nontrivial victories for compassion and justice.

Additionally, Marty's quasi-reconciliation with his family shows Rust that a measure of forgiveness and understanding can be attained even after a long history of strained relationships. Rust also finds that he can take some comfort in knowing that his daughter did not suffer at the end of her short life.

Rust's Conversion

There are intimations of an afterlife in the final scene of the first season, and some sublime meditations on the starry night sky, to be sure, but in the end it does not seem that Rust's conversion is theological in nature. Rather, I interpret his final turn as resulting from the realization that some degree of affirmation is warranted by the empirical evidence. In other words, he realizes that thoroughgoing pessimism and resignation from life is not an intellectually honest stance to take. In light of his epistemic shift, he might even come to the view that his former resignation might be positively immoral, but Rust's character arc, with the series, ends only with the former, more ecumenical realization.

So, Rust's character throughout the series goes from (1) self-described jaded, wannabe-suicidal pessimist who belies his own self-understanding by energetically fighting crime to (2) one who really embraces that self-description, resigns from life, and aims to drink himself to death to (3) the cautious affirmer of life through compassionate engagement with the world. Rust finds some grounds for hope, and he chooses to continue on the path of compassion and justice, the path to try to improve the world. This prompts the question of whether he ever really embraced suicide in principle, and just lacked the constitution to pull it off, or whether, like Schopenhauer, he perhaps always found the intellectual grounds for such a radical decision to be shaky. At the very least, we can conclude that, as the eponymous "true detective," he was duty-bound to pursue the evidence—evidence for hope or lack thereof—wherever it would lead.

Notes

1. An earlier version of this chapter originally appeared online at *The Critique*.

2. Arthur Schopenhauer, *The World as Will and Representation*, vol. 2, trans. R. B. Haldane and J. Kemp (London: Routledge & Kegan, 1957), 578. First printed 1883.
3. Arthur Schopenhauer, "Prize Essay on the Basis of Morals," in *The Two Fundamental Problems of Ethics*, trans. and ed. Christopher Janaway (New York: Cambridge University Press, 2009), 162.
4. "True Detective Season 1: Inside the Episode #8 (HBO)." *YouTube*, March 9, 2014. https://www.youtube.com/watch?v=cE2n-nwiqDs.
5. Arthur Schopenhauer, *The World as Will and Representation*, vol. 1, trans. and ed. Judith Norman, Alistair Welchman, and Christopher Janaway (New York: Cambridge University Press, 2010), sec. 69, 426. German original: *Die Welt als Wille und Vorstellung* (Zürich: Haffsmans Verlag, 1988).
6. Schopenhauer, *World as Will and Representation*, vol. 1, 426–427.
7. Ibid., 428.
8. Rüdiger Safranski, *Schopenhauer and the Wild Years of Philosophy*, trans. Ewald Iosers (London: Weidenfeld & Nicolson, 1989), 105.
9. Ibid., 218.
10. Ibid., fn. 230.
11. Ibid., 231.

Grounding Carcosa
Cosmic Horror and Philosophical Pessimism in *True Detective*

Christopher Mountenay

Like many fans of *True Detective*, I was somewhat disappointed with the season one finale, "Form and Void." It was definitely not a bad hour of television, but it undid much of the work that the first seven episodes had done. "Form and Void" both diminished the element of cosmic horror into something more terrestrial and mundane and replaced Rust Cohle's trademark philosophical pessimism with a metaphysical optimism.

"This Is Some Halloween Shit"

Let's clarify what we mean by cosmic horror, supernatural horror, or weird fiction.[1] Most horror fiction that the West consumes consists either of familiar folkloric archetypes or completely naturalistic violence. The former is often only frightening to children because the familiarity of, say, vampires and werewolves makes them into easy objects of self-parody for most people. The latter includes subgenres such as slasher films, which rely on scenarios that, while typically outlandish, are at least physically possible. Partisans of this type of horror will argue that it is the scariest since it could "really happen."

Cosmic horror takes the opposite approach. A tale of cosmic horror will typically, but not always, begin with elements that seem

True Detective and Philosophy: A Deeper Kind of Darkness, First Edition.
Edited by Jacob Graham and Tom Sparrow.
© 2018 John Wiley & Sons Ltd. Published 2018 by John Wiley & Sons Ltd.

"realistic" but then veer into things that are impossible, at least from a rationalistic, naturalistic perspective. Yet what makes these things scary is not that they can occur in the realm of possibility but that they actually alter our understanding of what is possible. The master of this style, H. P. Lovecraft (1890–1937), in his long essay *Supernatural Horror in Literature*, describes it as follows:

> This type of fear-literature must not be confounded with a type externally similar but psychologically widely different; the literature of mere physical fear and the mundanely gruesome. ... These things are not the literature of cosmic fear in its purest sense. The true weird tale has something more than secret murder, bloody bones, or a sheeted form clanking chains according to rule. A certain atmosphere of breathless and unexplainable dread of outer, unknown forces must be present; and there must be a hint, expressed with a seriousness and portentousness becoming its subject, of that most terrible conception of the human brain—a malign and particular suspension or defeat of those fixed laws of Nature which are our only safeguard against the assaults of chaos and the daemons of unplumbed space.[2]

Lovecraft's form of horror is not concerned with "physical fear." The fear of death, even a violent death, is not what Lovecraft is trying to invoke. Rather, he sees the "oldest" and "strongest" fear to be the "fear of the unknown."[3] Lovecraft fears the "hidden and fathomless worlds of strange life which may pulsate in the gulfs beyond the stars, or press hideously upon our own globe in unholy dimensions which only the dead and the moonstruck can glimpse."[4]

A typical Lovecraft story involves a protagonist discovering some oddity, investigating it, and then watching his world unravel as eldritch horrors are awoken and a secret history of the world is unearthed. The protagonist of the story begins in a state of relative naïveté, not understanding the secret nature of the world and thinking that things ultimately make sense. While Rust is an exception to this trope, Marty Hart, despite his rough exterior, is such a character. In "The Long Bright Dark" he describes himself as "just a regular dude with a big-ass dick." Marty proclaims his Christian faith and is horrified by Rust's philosophical views. We also see the value that he places on his family and his libido, though the two are at odds. As the season continues, Marty's faith in all of these things is shaken, though perhaps not to the point that one would expect from a cosmic horror story. Though Lovecraft's protagonists tend to be nebbish antiquarians and academics, not all protagonists of cosmic horror tales are squeamish. In fact, some of the best cosmic horror stories of the early twenty-first century, namely those by Laird Barron, feature protagonists displaying Marty's style of machismo. The lesson that they often learn, though, is that even such fortitude is ultimately futile in the face of cosmic horror.[5] The best-case scenario in most works of cosmic horror is that the monstrosity that was unveiled goes back to sleep. All too often, though, heroes learn that the horrors they face are not only very real but also deeply woven into their own identity.

The horror is based not around the fear of what the monster can do to us but rather around *the very fact that there are monsters.* This is what separates cosmic horror from fantasy. A story involving monsters, such as *The Lord of the Rings* or the Harry Potter books, is not necessarily a horror story. A fantasy story typically presents the existence of monsters as a matter of fact. The characters react to the revelation of the existence of ghosts and goblins in the same way that a reader of a science magazine might react to the discovery of a new species of lizard: possibly with interest, but nothing life-defining. The reason is that no new philosophical questions are raised by the existence of the paranormal. If there are talking animals, what does that say about our previously held notion of humans being the sole sapient species on earth? The existence of ghosts should both settle debates and open up new questions about the existence of life after death. Yet, in much fiction, these discoveries are treated in a blasé manner.

Cosmic horror works differently. Even if we may find Lovecraft's beautifully described monsters to be hokey, we must question the role of humans in the cosmos. Lovecraft's monsters are not malevolent. Rather, they are of the mindset that humanity is beneath consideration. Humanity is to them as insects are to us. This goes against the typical religious or humanist doctrines that see humanity as either the highest of God's creations or the pinnacle of evolution. If beings like Cthulhu or the Yellow King do exist, humanity's precarious place is threatened. If things exist that can violate the laws of nature, then how may we trust those laws? Lovecraft's description of these "safeguards" is apt. Modern science has been a candle in the dark, but cosmic horror blows that candle out.

Thomas Ligotti, a living master of cosmic horror, said that "in the right surroundings our entire being is made of eyes that dilate to witness the haunting of the universe."[6] And what is more horrific is that, once one's eyes have been opened to it, no light can chase it away, since "horror eats the light and digests it into darkness."[7] It's not the threat of being taken by the Green Man to be sacrificed to the Yellow King that should scare us when we watch and imagine the world of *True Detective*. What's truly scary is living in a world where such things exist and in which our very sense of self is permeated with that darkness. Why would someone enjoy such imaginings? The simple answer is that we like to be scared. But Ligotti proposes something darker. Some of us already have the sort of philosophical inklings that someone like Rust has, and by personifying them and making a spectacle of them, as we do when we read cosmic horror, we're allowed to step outside ourselves and enjoy the horror while not feeling it devours us.

Heroes of cosmic horror stories are changed by their experiences. At the beginning of the story, they are optimistic and have faith in the rational, but by the end they are filled with dread and find little value in anything. This is what makes Rust Cohle such an interesting protagonist: he begins the story pessimistic and nihilistic. It's as if he has already been through the horror and is now attempting to live a relatively human life. He is irrevocably changed, though, and others can sense it. Even the meth cook Dewall can see Rust's internal corruption: the "corrosive" demon that is inside him.

"It Means I'm Bad at Parties"

The jarring feeling that horror gives us is hard to replicate without putting ourselves in actual danger. The closest most of us will get is taking Philosophy 101. Yet the closest feeling we can have to that of a cosmic horror protagonist is being a philosopher. Many students complain that the class is like something out of a horror movie, and they might be on to something. In both the film and the class, people start out with a feeling that the world makes perfect sense but then start asking questions and finding faults with the worldview that most people passively accept. Comforting illusions dissipate and the unfamiliar and alien become much closer.[8]

Luckily, most philosophers give us back a world of rationality, sometimes more rational than the one they wrenched from us. But there are others who leave us with the feeling of horror, such as the German philosopher Arthur Schopenhauer (1788–1860), who is notorious for disrupting people's happy worlds. Schopenhauer was a sort of prototype for Rust Cohle: brooding, argumentative, sharp-tongued, but not without basic decency. The philosophy that he laid out, in his magnum opus *The World as Will and Representation*, is recognizable to any fan of *True Detective*. It's characterized by both a pessimistic worldview and a will-based metaphysics, both hallmarks of Rust's personal philosophy.

The conversation in the car between Rust and Marty in the first episode of season one is practically a beginners' guide to Schopenhauer. It's sparked by Rust asserting that the world is "all one ghetto, man ... a giant gutter in outer space." Schopenhauer was, if anything, less positive about the world, declaring it to be a "Hell" and saying that humans "are the tortured souls on the one hand, and the devils on the other."[9] Rust adds that "human consciousness was a tragic misstep in evolution" and that "we are creatures that should not exist." Again, this is an idea that Schopenhauer explored at great length, arguing that life is a "uselessly disturbing episode in the blessed repose of nothingness."[10] The following quotation by Schopenhauer could have been inserted into any episode of *True Detective* as one of Rust's lines and I doubt the audience would have noticed any tonal shift:

> If we picture to ourselves roughly as far as we can the sum total of misery, pain, and suffering of every kind on which the sun shines in its course, we shall admit that it would have been much better if it had been just as impossible for the sun to produce the phenomenon of life on earth as on the moon, and the surface of the earth, like that of the moon, had still been in a crystalline state.[11]

Rust echoes these lines, saying that the best thing for human beings to do would be to "deny our programming," "stop reproducing," and "walk hand in hand into extinction." The notion of being preprogrammed to reproduce appears in Schopenhauer's work as the manifestation of the unthinking will-to-live. Decades before Darwin's theory, Schopenhauer imagined an inborn force in all of us that wishes for our species to survive and procreate. The trap through which this will-to-live catches us is the sexual impulse. We are driven by the pleasures of sex to reproduce, albeit accidentally. Like Rust, Schopenhauer thinks it's programming that we have to deny if we want to escape the horrors of the world.[12] In fact, Schopenhauer denies the existence of any higher intelligences elsewhere in the world, as any beings more intelligent than us, if they were truly that intelligent, would have already committed species-wide suicide.[13] Here Schopenhauer refers to intelligence as the means for "imparting to the will that knowledge in consequence of which the will denies and abolishes itself."[14] The will makes itself known to itself, just as Rust says self-awareness is the aspect of nature that nature makes to be separate from itself.

A similar biographical element links Rust and Schopenhauer: both had daughters who died very young. Schopenhauer said practically nothing about his daughter, though his sister was crushed about the death of her niece, seeing her as a potential source of joy in her brother's gloomy life.[15] Rust, on the other hand, does meditate on his daughter's death in, perhaps, the most crushing of his monologues. He describes how his daughter died, painlessly slipping into nonexistence, and he envies her dying as a happy child, mostly unaware of the pain of life. Then he issues a condemnation of the very act of parenting itself: "Think of the hubris it must take to yank a soul out of nonexistence into this ... meat, to force a life into this ... thresher. That's ... so my daughter, she spared me the sin of being a father." Schopenhauer would have agreed. He saw procreation as something that we should naturally be ashamed of and that we would never knowingly inflict on another. That is why the will finds it necessary to blind us.[16]

Yanking a soul out of nonexistence and forcing it into "meat" is a very Schopenhauerian way to describe birth. He describes it this way:

> Awakened to life out of the night of unconsciousness, the will finds itself as an individual in an endless and boundless world, among innumerable individuals, all striving, suffering, and erring; and, as if through a troubled dream, it hurries back to the old unconsciousness. Yet till then its desires are unlimited, its claims inexhaustible, and every desire gives birth to a new one.[17]

Again, we see the use of the word "will" to describe the inner self. Rust uses the same word when he describes the "dream of being a person" in the episode "The Locked Room." He recognizes a "person" as being a "jerry-rig of presumption and dumb will." For both Rust and Schopenhauer, this will is dreaming that it is a person. The will in Schopenhauer's sense is the essential nature of the person, of all things.[18] All of the other aspects, such as intellect and personality, are fleeting illusions. The will is that part of things that cannot be made an object of representation. The will is the anonymous nobody that Rust is talking about when he says that we're all pretending to "be somebody." It is a blind striving that is never satisfied but continues to create new beings who act as masks for it.

"Time Is a Flat Circle"

The pedophilic cultist Ledoux delivers the most memorable philosophical musing that came out of *True Detective*. "Time is a flat circle," he tells Rust, who recognizes the quote from Friedrich Nietzsche (1844–1900). Indeed, Nietzsche himself said that his greatest contribution to philosophy was the notion of the eternal return—that is to say, the idea that everything that has happened will repeat itself in the exact same way an infinite number of times.[19] But Nietzsche was not the first to conceive of eternal repetition; the ancient Greeks had described such an idea.

What Rust describes for the interviewing detectives, Gilbough and Papania, about the M-theory is in fact a very Schopenhauerian concept:

> It's like in this universe we process time linearly forward. But outside of our space-time from what would be a fourth dimensional perspective time wouldn't exist. And from that vantage could we attain it? We see ... [Rust crushes a can] our space-time would look flattened. Like a single sculpture of matter and super-position of every place it ever occupied. Our sentience is just cycling through our lives like carts on a track. See everything outside our dimension that's eternity. Eternity looking down on us. Now to us it's a sphere but to them it's a circle.

In Schopenhauer's philosophy, time and space are faculties for pro-
cessing the world, but they do not exist in and of themselves. The
will itself is eternal and boundless, totally outside space and time.
We perceive time as constantly in the present, the past slipping into
oblivion and the future nonexistent, but it also seems to be moving
continuously forward. Schopenhauer says that:

> We can compare time to an endlessly revolving sphere; the half that
> is always sinking would be the past, and the half that is always rising
> would be the future; but at the top, the indivisible point that touches
> the tangent would be the extensionless present"[20]

The will, as outside of time, or eternal, would see the whole of the
sphere, not just its present.[21]

The horror of eternity, a cosmic horror if there ever was one,
truly dawns on Rust as he contemplates the consequences of the
repetition of time.

> In eternity, where there is no time, nothing can grow. Nothing can
> become. Nothing changes. So death created time to grow the things
> that it would kill … and you are reborn but into the same life that
> you've always been born into. I mean, how many times have we had
> this conversation, detectives? Well, who knows? When you can't
> remember your lives, you can't change your lives, and that is the
> terrible and the secret fate of all life. You're trapped … like a night-
> mare you keep waking up into.

The horror of the will is that it is eternal, so it needs to manifest itself temporally in order to satisfy its constant strivings. It is
ultimately never satisfied, though, and so indefinitely continues the
meaningless farce of time. There's nothing really outside it, so we're
all doomed to repeat what it inflicts upon itself an infinite number
of times. Even in the best of circumstances, this is maddening, but
Rust focuses especially on the children whom he and Marty rescued
from Ledoux. Even if they're safe from Ledoux "now," they'll have
to experience the torture they suffered under him an infinite number of times, and there's nothing anyone can do to prevent that.

"The Light Is Winning"

The philosophical underpinnings of both Rust and Schopenhauer are those of horror. Both have peeled back the veil of everyday existence and found something sinister underneath, namely a blind, irrational will that lurks at the center of everyone and everything. While Schopenhauer saw this as apparent from his readings of history and science, later authors have used the genre of cosmic horror to express those same ideas, as I've explained. When Lovecraft talks of his Elder Gods or Ligotti summons the Shadow at the Bottom of the World, they're not being literal. Both men have crafted the monsters out of a fear of this inhuman weirdness that lurks at the edge of things. Finding out that the world is secretly run by monsters is a metaphorical way of describing one's realization of pessimistic philosophy. What once made sense now doesn't.

And, if *True Detective* had ended after seven episodes, this would have been the takeaway. Instead, the cosmic horror and pessimistic philosophy are undermined by the final acts of "Form and Void," the finale. First, the Yellow King, Carcosa, and the Green Man are all revealed as "ordinary" occurrences. This isn't to say that cults, child molesters, and serial killers aren't frightening. But, if one were to ask one's most cheerful, optimistic friends if such things existed, they would have to say "yes." In other words, such things are already a given for any person living in the modern world. No new philosophies need to be developed, since we've already made room for such things. They don't ask us to reevaluate our world on any metaphysical level; they just add an extra tragedy or two to our preexisting systems. The motivations of the villains weren't really occult; that is to say, nothing was hidden, at least nothing true. When the mystery of Carcosa is unraveled, it doesn't reveal anything besides the disconnect with reality of the cultists. Our world is untouched.

But the real betrayal to the pessimism and cosmic horror of *True Detective* comes from Rust himself. When he has his final vision, he experiences the presence of his daughter, who earlier in the series he had been happy to consign to oblivion. He's comforted by her continued existence, and that of his father, whereas earlier he had seen existence as a mistake. This relief at presence rather than at oblivion is a way of communicating that he has come to see the world as having value; it is better to be than not to be. He could have slipped into nonexistence, but he is kept in existence by the force of love. His father's and daughter's love for him has survived (not their blind will). This is obviously not the sort of ending that Lovecraft or Ligotti would ever put in a story.

Even worse, from a pessimistic perspective, is Rust's commentary on the stars. He describes the night sky as an illustration of the oldest of conflicts: that of light versus dark, with stars as light and sky as void. Marty correctly notes that it looks as though the dark is winning, but Rust corrects him by saying that the light is winning, since in the beginning there was only dark. I don't want to take away from the beauty of this exchange, but it is the reversal of the pessimistic cosmology of Schopenhauer. He would never want us to put hope in the future, but Rust is saying that positive change, albeit small and incremental, is coming. And there's an even deeper conflict with Schopenhauer's worldview concerning the linearity of time. If time is indeed a flat circle, then any change is ultimately fruitless; things will end up back where they started. Indeed, from the standpoint of eternity, all that has happened and will happen is present. Change isn't possible because change requires time, and there is no time within which change can occur. Rust has abandoned Schopenhauer's pessimistic theory of time in favor of a view that many Westerners hold: that the future will be better due to either progress or otherworldly salvation.

True Detective demonstrated real bravery by having a character like Rust Cohle, but I see the ending as a compromise. A darker ending would have been unnerving for most people. While Lovecraft, Ligotti, and Schopenhauer all eventually found audiences, they never had the huge audience of an HBO hit show. So giving the mass audience even a taste of pessimism and cosmic horror was daring. It's too bad that, at the last minute, the show backed off and Carcosa merely became a place on earth.

Notes

1. I will use the terms relatively interchangeably but will predominantly use "cosmic horror" since it is the most precise.
2. H. P. Lovecraft, *The Annotated Supernatural Horror in Literature*, ed. S. T. Joshi (New York: Hippocampus, 2012), 27–28.

3. Ibid., 25.
4. Ibid., 27.
5. Notable examples of Barron's use of this theme include "Bulldozer," "The Broadsword," and "Blackwood's Baby," found in the collections *The Imago Sequence* (New York: Night Shade Books, 2008), *Occultation and Other Stories* (New York: Night Shade Books, 2010), and *The Beautiful Thing that Awaits Us All* (New York: Night Shade Books, 2014), respectively.
6. Thomas Ligotti, "Professor Nobody's Little Lectures on Horror," in *Songs of a Dead Dreamer and Grimscribe* (New York: Penguin, 2015), 183.
7. Ibid., 184.
8. Eugene Thacker, *Tentacles Longer than Night: Horror of Philosophy*, vol. 3 (Croydon: Zero Books, 2015).
9. Arthur Schopenhauer, *Parerga and Paralipomena: Short Philosophical Essays*, vol. 2, trans. E. F. J. Payne (Oxford: Oxford University Press, 1974), 300.
10. Ibid., 299.
11. Ibid.
12. Arthur Schopenhauer, *The World as Will and Representation*, vol. 2, trans. E. F. J. Payne (New York: Dover, 1969), 568.
13. Ibid., 610.
14. Ibid.
15. David Cartwright, *Schopenhauer: A Biography* (Cambridge: Cambridge University Press, 2010), 344.
16. Schopenhauer, *World as Will and Representation*, vol. 2, 568.
17. Ibid., 573.
18. Ibid., 230.
19. Friedrich Nietzsche, "Why I Write Such Good Books: *Thus Spoke Zarathustra*," trans. Walter Kaufmann, in *On the Genealogy of Morals and Ecce Homo*, ed. Walter Kaufmann (New York: Vintage, 1967), secs. 1 and 6.
20. Arthur Schopenhauer, *The World as Will and Representation*, vol. 1, trans. E. F. J. Payne (New York: Dover, 1969), 279.
21. Ibid., 280.

Hart and Cohle
The Hopeful Pessimism of *True Detective*[1]

Joshua Foa Dienstag

In one of the first scenes of the *True Detective* pilot episode "The Long Bright Dark," detective Rust Cohle is being badgered by his partner Marty Hart about his beliefs. Much to Marty's surprise, Rust denies being a Christian, and when Marty presses further Rust says, "I consider myself a realist, all right, but in philosophical terms, I'm what's called a pessimist." When Marty asks what that means, Rust blows him off with the line, "It means I'm bad at parties."

But what *does* it mean to be a pessimist? And, more importantly, why would anyone, especially a detective, want to be one? In the scene, Rust goes on to give a bit of explanation, but the key is the little phrase "in philosophical terms."

What Pessimism Is and Is Not

Ordinarily, when we use the words "optimist" and "pessimist," we intend them as a description of personality. Optimists are cheerful and forward-looking people; pessimists are morose downers. And, indeed, there are various personality types in the world, people who are habitually happy or unhappy.

But when philosophers use the words "optimistic" and "pessimistic" they mean something else—something that has nothing

True Detective and Philosophy: A Deeper Kind of Darkness, First Edition.
Edited by Jacob Graham and Tom Sparrow.
© 2018 John Wiley & Sons Ltd. Published 2018 by John Wiley & Sons Ltd.

to do with disposition. To a philosopher, it is *ideas* that are optimistic or pessimistic. Cohle may be gloomy, but, when he claims to be a pessimist, it's not a personality trait that he is talking about at all.

In the philosophical tradition, someone is an optimist or a pessimist based on their ideas about how the world hangs together (or fails to) in a basic way. Optimists are people (such as Plato and Kant) who think there is a fundamental order to the universe that the human mind can grasp. Pessimists are people (such as Schopenhauer and Nietzsche) who don't. No doubt there are philosophers who mix the two perspectives or who escape the categories altogether, but for the purposes of this chapter it will be useful to consider what makes these two sets of ideas distinctive.

Many contrasting worldviews are optimistic—those of the devout Christian and the atheist scientist are equally so. They both think the universe is governed by clear laws (just different ones) that we can all understand. Even if there are some particular things that are unknown or mysterious, the basic structure is something we can all get our head around. It was for just this reason that Friedrich Nietzsche (1844–1900), for example, identified modern science with the Christianity and Platonism it appeared to reject.[2] What all three shared, according to Nietzsche, was a belief that the world's rules were comprehensible to the human mind through its faculty of reason.

When you know the basic laws of the universe, whether through Platonic deduction or scientific induction, you are in a good position to make your life better and you have good reason to expect to succeed. You're in the driver's seat, so to speak, even before you choose a destination. That is why, from Nietzsche's perspective, you are a philosophical *optimist* if you think like this. Regardless of whether or not you are constitutionally cheerful, you believe you have the tools to conduct your life agreeably.

But there is a long line of philosophers who deny that the universe is like this or that we have, in the faculty of reason, any kind of power over it. In the original script for *True Detective* (in a line that didn't make it onto the screen), Cohle mentions Arthur Schopenhauer (1788–1860), probably the most famous of these philosophical pessimists.[3] But he is not the only one: Nietzsche, Miguel de Unamuno (1864–1936), Albert Camus (1913–1960), and many others can be gathered together under the banner of pessimism. What the pessimists share is not a substantive ethics or metaphysics but rather a skepticism that the relation between human reason and the laws of nature (if any) can be as direct as the optimists believe.[4]

Although Schopenhauer, for example, took himself to be a student of Immanuel Kant (1724–1804), he was merciless about the idea that there was an order in this world for the mind to discover. Kant, he believed, had failed to draw the proper conclusions from his own metaphysics. Space and time, Kant had argued, were concepts fundamental for our grasp of the world. But the very constitutional quality of time, for Schopenhauer, made the world itself unstable and thus, to his way of thinking, unknowable in any substantive sense:

> *Time* and the *perishability* of all things existing in time that time itself brings about is simply the form under which the will to live … reveals to itself the vanity of its striving. Time is that by virtue of which everything becomes nothingness in our hands and loses all real value.[5]

Living in a time-bound world means that no object in that world is eternal. What Schopenhauer maintains here is not much more than the idea that nothing lasts forever—but he includes not only physical objects but also relationships, institutions, and values, even those that seem to us the most solid or everlasting, such as love and honor. Whether we desire wealth, power, or love, we can only achieve such things temporarily. So we will have to suffer the pain of losing whatever we gain and, more importantly, the pain of knowing that all of our achievements are ultimately insubstantial and our efforts came to nothing. While one could argue (and Schopenhauer did) that there is a worthwhile knowledge to be had in understanding that your goals and possessions won't last, that conclusion by itself will not be of much comfort to most of us who would like something of substance to show for our lives.

And, if that was not enough, Nietzsche, in turn, ridiculed Schopenhauer's continued adherence to traditional morality and insisted on abandoning Kant's metaphysics entirely. But Nietzsche's own view of the world retained the idea that the attempt to mentally master it through reason was a fool's errand:

> This world: a monster of energy, without beginning, without end ...
> a sea of forces flowing and rushing together, eternally changing,
> eternally flooding back ... a becoming that knows no satiety, no
> disgust, no weariness: this [is] my *Dionysian* world of the eternally
> self-creating, the eternally self-destroying ... without goal, unless
> the joy of the circle is itself a goal.[6]

When Cohle, in his famous drunken oration to the uncompre-
hending police detectives in episode five, declares that "time is
a flat circle," it is hard not to hear an echo of this Nietzschean
metaphysics (or anti-metaphysics). The world repeats itself, but,
whatever laws it might obey (if any), they are not such that the
human mind can grasp or predict them. It is circular in the sense
that it is not progressing (morally or scientifically) toward any goal
but rather endlessly repeating an interaction of forces that we label
good and evil in order to make sense of them. Not that the world
cares about our labels. "Time is a flat circle" means that the world
goes nowhere as a whole (neither up nor down); the same circumstances recur in different guises. As in Schopenhauer, the power of
time means that the world is not ours to master or remake; we can
only marvel at its chaos and dynamism.

At one level, the pessimists have little in common with one
another. Schopenhauer was an (unusual) Kantian; Nietzsche was
an anti-Kantian. Camus was an atheist; Unamuno a (unusual)
Catholic. But, just as the optimists share the idea that the universe
is a fundamentally *ordered* place, the pessimists share the idea that
the universe is a fundamentally *disordered* or *contradictory* place,
at least from any perspective that a human being could hope to
achieve.[7] Pessimism is not a belief that things will get *worse*, either
for the individual or the species—it is more profoundly a rejection
of the idea that the universe has laws that can be grasped, that
"it will all make sense in the end."

If our world can never be fully described by any law that humans
can know, then we cannot be its masters, either intellectually or in
practice. We cannot successfully predict its patterns or the effects of
our actions, which means that even the most powerful individuals
must live with unintended consequences and tragedies. For Cohle,

this was brought home by the death of his daughter, whom he loved more than anything, and the end of his marriage, which could not survive the tragedy despite the goodwill of himself and his wife.

That the world is chaotic is not something the pessimist *enjoys* or *wants*; they suffer from this situation just like anyone else. But it is something the pessimist feels bound to acknowledge. Although this is not the kind of knowledge that creates control over circumstances, as the optimist claims to possess, it is knowledge nonetheless. Would you want, for example, a weathercaster who predicted the weather as they would *like it to be* or as it *actually is*? We do not control the weather—but knowledge of its power at least allows us to get out of the way of terrible storms or to hunker down to survive them. Worse still than an optimistic weathercaster would be a forecaster who actually believed their knowledge of meteorology meant they could control what happens.

To pessimists, optimists have the *illusion* that they have mastery over their lives. We keep *believing* that we have the power to make our lives better, even in the face of all our failures to do so. No technology, morality, or foresight protects us from death and change, and even the shiniest new toy will eventually rust (as Cohle's name indicates). But the optimist can, in effect, multiply the damage we all will suffer by adding illusions on top of the situation. When these illusions are pierced, it adds the pain of disappointment to the more mundane pains that time inflicts by itself. So, to the pessimist, optimism is not just blind but, to a point, dangerous.

In *True Detective*, this optimism is embodied in Rust's partner, Marty. Marty has everything that Rust lacks—a happy and loving family, stability, and, apparently, a bright future as a policeman. But, by the end of the first season, it will be clear that Marty has lost all of these. They are lost through a combination of historical circumstance (the slow decline of white supremacy, instantiated by the black detectives who are now investigating *him*) and Marty's own recklessness and insatiable habits (sex, booze, etc.). Through it all, until the final episode, Marty keeps imagining that he is in control of his situation and that his intelligence and good attitude will preserve his fortune. Only by the very end does he come to the realization that Rust may have been right all along. And only then can a real friendship between the two detectives finally take hold.

Pessimism, Freedom, and Truth

Why be a pessimist? Well, who is most likely to be satisfied over the long term? Why are we constantly surprised when things don't work out the way we plan? How many people do you know who succeed in getting everything they aim at? And how many are happy when, by some great good fortune, they do?

Optimism sets us up for perpetual disappointment. We set goals for our careers and our personal lives that hardly ever come to pass, and even when they do come to pass we may find, to our surprise, that they are not what we wanted after all or they don't give the pleasure or satisfaction we expected. And then, even if they do, we cannot hold onto these goods and must make up for the pain of their loss by chasing after new goals, only to find ourselves, treadmill-like, repeating the process.

Pessimism, by contrast, prepares us for a world that is constantly changing and surprising us. It tells us to banish our expectations and the illusion that we are in control of our destiny. It allows us, in fact, to stop measuring our lives against some impossible plan that we fail to live up to.

In that sense, pessimism is a kind of freedom to take each day as it comes and to be grateful for the good that occasionally appears, whether or not it fits any plan. The pessimist is rarely disappointed for the simple reason that they have no expectations to disappoint. When good things happen, they can be recognized for the lucky, happy circumstance that they are, rather than being trivialized as the expected outcome of a personal plan or a fixed historical trajectory. Pessimism may seem like a harsh perspective but, in practice, it turns out to be a beneficent one.

Pessimism is also the reason that Rust is a better detective than Marty. Rust has no preconceptions of what he will find, so he is more attentive to details that others miss. He is not surprised by and he does not judge the people he encounters, so he makes fewer mistakes in sizing them up. Marty thinks he knows how the world works, but his image of how things should be keeps getting in the way of his seeing how they actually are. He is deceived by illusions of his own making. Rust may have had this problem once, but, having given up his optimism, he is never shocked by the depravity that he encounters as the investigation unfolds.

Most fundamentally, Rust does not expect to encounter rationality and law in his investigation of the world. He is a better guide to its basic lawlessness. To be a "true detective" means to be able to detect what is true. The pessimist, with fewer illusions than the optimist, is the best possible detective, even if they are not a good party guest or a good "lawman."

Rust ultimately leaves the police, because, I would say, his knowledge of the world's lawlessness makes his enforcement of human-made "law" feel like a joke to him. This has nothing to do with his sense of right and wrong or good and evil, which remain entirely intact. But to expect the world, or other people, to conform to law is hopelessly optimistic and ultimately futile. By the end of the season (and the same pattern happens in the second season though the trajectory is different), both Rust and Marty, while remaining detectives, are operating well outside the law and, indeed, in defiance of the legal institutions and police that surround them.

The police themselves (in the first season anyway) are not irredeemably corrupt; they simply cannot comprehend the wickedness that surrounds them because they remain blinded by their own illusions. The perpetrators of the various crimes under investigation are less criminal masterminds than profoundly evil individuals who walk around in plain sight unnoticed. Rust and Marty do not apprehend them or bring them to justice—that is, they do not really succeed in enforcing the law. Rather, the two detectives kill their opponents and escape with their lives in a lucky encounter that they were in no way fated to win.

Optimists are not bad people. But they are not effective truth seekers and they are prone to disappointment. At the end of *True Detective*, Marty, who began with a family and a promising career, has neither. Rust, who had nothing and expected nothing, has gained a friend. Pessimistic freedom may have few pleasures but it is at least clear-eyed about what (little) we can expect from this world.

Pessimism and Hope

Optimism and pessimism do not exhaust the characters Rust and Marty: "Hart and Cohle" sounds too much like "heart and soul" to be a coincidence. Before their final encounter with the sadistic murderer they have been pursuing, Rust Cohle is at the point of giving up. His pessimism has shriveled into hopelessness and despair. Marty Hart, for all his obtuseness about the world (and himself), does have something to contribute to his partner—a willingness to keep hope alive.

In everyday speech we conflate hope and optimism (and despair and pessimism). We believe that these terms must remain wedded to one another. But in a sense the pairing of detectives Hart and Cohle is meant to demonstrate that this is not so. Cohle's despair is *not* the result of his pessimism per se but of the particular tragic loss of his family, which, though terrible, he has survived. Hart, too, has survived the destruction of all his plans and the basis of his optimism. But his attitude remains positive and, in the final scenes, he effectively brings Cohle back to life after he nearly dies.

To put it crudely, hope and despair are attitudes whereas optimism and pessimism are ideas. We may have an instinct that the attitudes derive from the ideas in a fixed way, but that instinct is wrong or, at least, not necessarily right. In fact, we can remain hopeful pessimists even if it is an unusual posture or a difficult one to achieve. Pessimism is not in any way a deterministic philosophy. Indeed, it leaves the future radically open. Recognizing that pessimism does not predict a necessary tragedy, we can understand that the relationship of attitude to idea is also open and that there is no requirement that the pessimist despair. We cannot choose our world or our future, but we can choose our attitude toward the world in which we find ourselves.

There is a great deal of difference between hope and expectation. Expectation is a faith or probabilistic belief that the future will produce some particular outcome. Hope, however, is a will not to lose faith in the possibility of goodness and a better future. There is nothing in hope that pessimism precludes or forbids. Indeed, Nietzsche recommended cheerfulness, along with pessimism, in the firm belief that there was no contradiction between the two. It may be that hope is easier to sustain in combination with optimism but that does not mean it is impossible for a pessimistic mind to sustain it also. It just may take more effort.

Hope and pessimism go together like heart and soul. Pessimism is a kind of insight and knowledge that helps us detect the truth.

Hope is an attitude that allows us to live with what we find when we do so. Hope without pessimism leads to delusion; pessimism without hope might lead to suicide. But they can be united in a productive partnership. At least, that is what I take to be the aim of *True Detective*'s first season: to portray an image of the life-affirming union of affect and knowledge in alignment with the well-established tenets of the pessimistic tradition.

Notes

1. An earlier version of this chapter originally appeared online at *The Critique*.
2. Friedrich Nietzsche, *The Gay Science* (New York: Vintage Books, 1974), Book 3.
3. Nic Pizzolatto, "The Long Bright Dark," p. 18. http://www.pages. drexel.edu/~ina22/splaylib/Screenplay-True%20Detective-Pilot.pdf.
4. My book *Pessimism: Philosophy, Ethic, Spirit* (Princeton: Princeton University Press, 2006) makes an argument for considering pessimism as a continuous intellectual tradition.
5. Arthur Schopenhauer, *Essays and Aphorisms* (New York: Penguin, 1970), 51.
6. Friedrich Nietzsche, *The Will to Power* (New York: Vintage, 1968), 550.
7. That is, some pessimists firmly believe that the universe is fundamentally disordered while others are more agnostic on this point and maintain only that, while laws might govern the universe, they are not laws that human reason is capable of grasping. But, from a practical perspective, they largely come down to the same thing.

Loving Rust's Pessimism

Rationalism and Emotion in *True Detective*

Rick Elmore

What motivates Rust Cohle's pessimism in the first season of *True Detective*? And what leads a person to be a pessimist at all? Is pessimism a principled philosophical position or the result of traumatic life experiences? The first season of *True Detective* offers conflicting answers to these questions. On the one hand, Rust's pessimism is linked to the tragic death of his daughter, implying that a profound, personal tragedy made him a pessimist. On the other hand, Rust never appeals to this tragedy or any other personal experience to justify his belief in the meaninglessness of existence, arguing always that it comes from a rational evaluation of reality. The question of to what degree pessimism is a principled, rational philosophy rather than a personal, affective perspective has been a major issue in recent work on pessimism.[1]

In particular, thinkers such as Joshua Foa Dienstag and Eugene Thacker argue that pessimism is a philosophical stance that can be usefully separated from personal psychology or perspectives, whereas pessimists such as Thomas Ligotti contend that pessimism is always a depressive and bleak "temperament" to which one is either born or not.[2] Does pessimism tell us something about the nature of all human life or does it only tell us something about how some experiences (suffering, for example) can negatively shape our perception of life? At stake in this question is whether pessimism

True Detective and Philosophy: A Deeper Kind of Darkness, First Edition.
Edited by Jacob Graham and Tom Sparrow.
© 2018 John Wiley & Sons Ltd. Published 2018 by John Wiley & Sons Ltd.

taps into something inherent within the nature of human life or is merely a fringe position of a few damaged individuals. However, this question also taps into the long-standing tendency in Western philosophy to contrast reason and emotion, objectivity and subjectivity, philosophical logic and personal experience.

"Boundaries Are Good"

In the history of Western philosophy, reason and emotion have often been opposed. In modern philosophy, this opposition is found, for example, in the influential debate between rationalism and empiricism. For rationalists, such as René Descartes (1596–1650), knowledge and truth are products of reason rather than experience; experience seems only able to give us limited impressions about how we happen to perceive reality and not necessarily knowledge of reality as it really is. For rationalists, reason is the faculty that allows humans to know and understand the logical structures of reality independently of experience. The philosopher, then, is the person who, through reason and deduction, follows out the inherent logic at work in reality.

In contrast to rationalists such as Descartes, empiricists, such as David Hume (1711–1776), argue that, despite the limited and unreliable nature of our experience, senses, and emotions, knowledge and truth can only come through experience, because experience is our only avenue for gathering any information about reality at all. For empiricists, sense experience is what provides our basic information about the world. The philosopher, then, is the one who sorts through the data provided by experience in order to deduce the nature of reality. Hence, the debate between rationalism and empiricism, like the debate over whether pessimism is a principled philosophy or personal worldview, is at root a debate about what role, if any, personal experience, feeling, and emotion ought to play in our philosophical thinking. Pessimists such as Dienstag take the more rationalist perspective, that it ought to have little to no role in philosophical pessimism. By contrast, pessimists such as Ligotti take the more empiricist position that personal experience has a necessary, even if problematic, role to play. In the context of the first season of *True Detective*, we see this debate played out in the relationship between Marty Hart and Rust Cohle.

Marty and Rust's partnership is one of the most entertaining aspects of the first season, the characters' witty and sarcastic exchanges making for some of the more memorable and quotable moments of the show. In addition, their partnership clearly associates their relationship with the debate between reason and emotion, rationalism and empiricism. More specifically, Marty embodies a person driven purely by personal experience and emotion. He is, as his last name suggests, all heart. He professes to be reasonable (to know all the rules, to be "steady," and to be good with people) yet always acts as though the rules do not apply to him personally. For example, despite insisting in "Who Goes There" on the importance of family as what "gives one boundaries," Marty is pathologically unable to stay within these boundaries. His infidelities and absence from his daughters' lives lead to the destruction of his family. Additionally, it is Marty who impulsively kills Reggie Ledoux after discovering the children imprisoned on Ledoux's compound, an act that undermines the chances of catching the real serial killer from the events that took place in 1995. Thus, despite his lip service to the importance of rules and boundaries, authority and family, reason and logic, Marty is, in fact, a man entirely directed by emotion and impulse. He is the embodiment of the rationalist's concern that, if you let personal experience and emotion have a role in your philosophical thinking, it will lead necessarily to contradictory, illogical, and damaging outcomes. In contrast to Marty, Rust is a character defined by a kind of rationalist adherence to logic and principle.

Despite being presented as a deeply damaged, antisocial drug abuser, Rust is, in practice, a profoundly rational and principled character (maybe the only truly principled character in the entire show). As he says in "Haunted Houses," he is a man who "knows exactly who he is" and refuses to compromise his character or principles for anyone. It is precisely this uncompromising honesty and clear-eyed objectivity that make Rust so good at getting confessions out of people, his ability to put his own feelings aside and "look at someone and think like they think" being the secret to his success as a "boxman" ("The Locked Room"). In addition, Rust repeatedly refuses to compromise his principles even when doing so would be to his advantage—for example, with his bosses at the precinct, with whom he constantly butts heads. Hence, Rust appears as a figure of reason and principle in contrast to Marty, who appears as a figure of impulse and emotion. This would seem to support the notion that not only Rust's character but also his pessimism are rationalisms based on reason and principle rather than empiricisms based on emotion and personal experience. However, one also sees Rust's rationalism in his arguments against religion.

"This World Is a Veil, and the Face You Wear Is Not Your Own"

Although many rationalist philosophers, such as Descartes, were religious, rationalism's focus on reason and logic over dogmatic faith and belief associates rationalism with secularism and, often, atheism, an association one also finds in *True Detective*. In "The Locked Room," having tracked Dora Lange's activities to the Friends of Christ ministry, Rust and Marty visit one of the congregation's tent revivals in order to question some of its members. In one of the most powerful scenes of the first season (and one of my personal favorites), they debate the function of religion in society and what this function tells us about the nature of human existence.

Rust opposes religion to reason, arguing that religion "dulls critical thinking" and hides the truth of existence from people: "What's it say about life," he questions Marty, "you gotta get together, tell yourself stories that violate every law of the universe just to get through the goddamn day?" What it tells Rust is that religion is a defense against the "fear and dread" of existence, encouraging people's "capacity for illusion" by selling them the hope that things will work out: "the ontological fallacy of expecting a light at the end of the tunnel, that's what the preacher sells." Religion falsely promises that, if we simply believe, we will be rewarded, and it can, therefore, promise us a meaningful existence. However, for Rust, if life really had a meaning that could be rationally shown, or if the suffering in our lives could be rationally justified, we would not need to tell ourselves improbable, illogical, and irrational stories in order to prove this meaning and justify our suffering. As he says in response to Marty's objections: "If the common good's gotta make up fairy tales, then it's not good for anyone." For Rust, religion is a problem because it stops us from being able to see and admit how things really are, replacing reason and facts with faith and beliefs, a concern implicit in rationalism's emphasis on reason.

In contrast to Rust's rationalist critique of religion, Marty defends religion as both an outlet for "community" and "the common good" and, most centrally, as a practical defense against the "freak show of murder and debauchery" that would ensue if people "didn't believe." Whether or not religion contains truth, for Marty, it serves a key role in controlling people's inherently base desires by making them feel like a part of something greater than themselves. It gives people rules and direction, without which, Marty is confident, they would act only in their own self-interest. Hence, for Marty, the importance of religion has little to do with truth and much more to do with the need to control people who are, like him, completely driven by their own selfish desires and feelings. Now, it is interesting that, in many ways, Marty's conception of human nature appears bleaker than Rust's. Marty sees humans as inherently selfish, violent creatures whereas Rust sees humans as victims of their own frailty and fear. Marty sees everything, including religion and Rust's attack on religion, as personally and emotionally motivated. Thus Marty's attack on Rust's critique of religion focuses on what he sees as Rust's elitism: "Can you see Texas from your high-horse? What do you know about these people?" In response to this accusation, Rust asserts again the rationalism of his position as "just observation and deduction," a logical analysis of the facts. Yet Marty sees Rust's account as personally motivated, a result of Rust's book-smart "fucking attitude." Again, Marty is associated with personal feelings and subjective attitudes whereas Rust is associated with depersonalized, objective rationalism. However, this rationalist orientation of Rust's character and critique of religion is also a central aspect of his pessimism.

"I Consider Myself a Realist"

In perhaps the most iconic scene of the first season, on the car ride back from the Dora Lange crime scene in "The Long Bright Dark," Rust explains his pessimism to Marty. Specifically, Rust believes that human life is something that "should not exist by natural law."

Evolution took a "tragic misstep" with the emergence of human consciousness, creating a form of self-awareness "separate" from the rest of nature. It is this separateness from nature that marks the paradox of "personhood" and human existence. For Rust, humans are creatures evolved to tragically experience themselves as something they are not, beings produced and determined by biological forces but who simultaneously see themselves as exceptions to those forces: "biological puppets" programmed to forget that they are puppets, as he says in "The Locked Room." For Rust, pessimism has nothing to do with personal disappointment, depression, or negativity; rather, pessimism is a logical response to the realities of human life and its evolutionary development. Rust emphasizes this point further by referring to himself as a "realist," someone who operates and thinks from the perspective of the objective reality of the world. Hence, in this initial account of his pessimism, Rust is clearly committed to the notion of pessimism as a rational philosophical position rather than a personal perspective, and the show's consistent characterization of Rust as the clear-eyed, principled, and rational figure in relation to Marty's rash impulsiveness further cements this picture. Hence, these scenes and the rational nature of Rust's character seem to support the picture of pessimism as an objective and rationalist position more than a subjective or personal perspective. Yet how does this characterization of pessimism deal with the prominent role the show also gives to personal tragedy, and, most centrally, the death of Rust's daughter?

"Was January the Third, My Daughter's Birthday, I Remember"

Toward the end of "Seeing Things," we get the story of how Rust's daughter was tragically killed when she was struck by a car while riding her tricycle:

> Sophia, my daughter. She was on her tricycle in our driveway. We lived down where'd a little bend in the road, and [... long silence]. They said that [... long silence]. Anyway, afterwards, Claire and I turned on each other, you know? We resented each other for being alive.

This event frames the first season of *True Detective* from beginning to end: the discovery of Dora Lange's body in episode one occurring on Sophia's birthday and Rust's apparent surrender to optimism in the show's finale, prompted by his near-death experience of her "love." In addition, this event paints a vivid picture of Rust as a deeply damaged individual who, in the wake of his child's death, throws himself into his work, loses his marriage, and is hospitalized after he "emptied a nine into a crankhead for injecting his infant daughter with crystal. Said he was trying to purify her." Hence, even though Rust is presented as a figure of reason and never appeals to his daughter's death as a justification for his pessimism, viewers are led from the beginning to connect her death and Rust's self-destructive behavior to his bleak view of existence. Insomnia, drug use, and his hesitancy to meet Marty's family are just the most outward signs of the havoc this event still wreaks on his life and the ways it forms his view of existence. Hence, the prominent role of Sophia's death seems to challenge the notion that Rust's pessimism is just the result of a rational philosophical account of reality. In fact, the symbolism of Sophia's death implies a fundamental separation between pessimism and philosophy as such.

"Sophia" is the Greek word for "wisdom" and is, etymologically, the root of the word "philosophy" ("love of wisdom"). Sophia is symbolically a figure of wisdom and philosophy in *True Detective*, and the prominent narrative role her death plays suggests that it is precisely the death or loss of wisdom and philosophy that is fundamentally at stake in Rust's pessimism. Following out this symbolism, Rust appears as the father of wisdom, suggesting a causal link between pessimism and philosophy: that one cannot be wise without first entertaining doubts about the meaningfulness of existence. On this reading, the relationship between Rust and Sophia presents pessimism as, symbolically, the father of philosophical wisdom, a notion that would seem to support the idea that Rust's pessimism is fundamentally philosophical. This emphasis on doubt as giving rise to philosophical thinking relates back to rationalism, the arch-rationalist philosopher Descartes insisting in the *Meditations* that philosophy must start by doubting all previous knowledge about the world.[3] However, in *True Detective* one cannot forget that it is Sophia's death, and symbolically therefore the death of wisdom and philosophy, that is at stake, suggesting that Rust's doubts about the meaningfulness of existence are, perhaps, less those of the father of wisdom and more a result of the loss of wisdom. This implication is powerfully brought home in the season finale, where it is Rust's experience of Sophia's "love"—which is to say, Rust's experience of the "love of wisdom" or philosophy—that leads him away from pessimism and back to the light of optimism. Hence, the symbolism of Sophia's death suggests that pessimism is not fundamentally philosophical (or about wisdom) but is the result of the death of philosophy (or loss of wisdom), a fact that challenges the reading of Rust's pessimism as a rationalist, philosophical position. Moreover, the rationalism of Rust's pessimism is further troubled by the fact that Sophia's death is the death of a child, and, for Rust, childhood implies a time of innocence before pessimism strikes.

"She Saved Me from the Sin of Being a Father"

Having detailed the event of Sophia's death and his time working deep undercover afterwards, Rust ponders the significance:

> I think about my daughter now, you know, what she was spared. Sometimes I feel grateful. Doctors said she didn't feel a thing. Went straight into a coma, and then, somewhere in that blackness, she slipped off into another, deeper kind. Isn't that a beautiful way to go out? Painlessly, as a happy child. Yeah, trouble with dying later is you've already grown up. Damage is done. It's too late. ("Seeing Things")

Rust has come to see his daughter's death as a kind of blessing, one that saved her from a life of suffering and saved him, as he goes on to say, from "the sin of being a father." Rust sees childhood as a time of innocence and beauty before one enters the damage and horror of existence, a "happy" time before the fall into suffering that constitutes growing up. Childhood is a time before one can doubt the meaninglessness of existence, the recognition of this meaninglessness requiring an experience of suffering and damage that, for Rust, Sophia thankfully avoided with her premature death. Now, putting aside whether Rust is right about the nature of childhood as a time of innocence, this characterization poses huge problems for understanding Rust's pessimism as a form of philosophical rationalism.

Remember that, for rationalists, philosophical knowledge ought not to rest fundamentally on experience but on logic and reason alone. However, for Rust, if one cannot understand pessimism or be a pessimist without experiencing the damage and suffering of "growing up," then it would follow that experience would be necessary for one to be a pessimist at all. On this reading, Rust's pessimism would have much more in common with empiricism rather than rationalism, insofar as experience, and particularly the experience of suffering, would be required for one to have pessimistic knowledge at all. Hence, the symbolism of Sophia's name and death, as well as Rust's characterization of childhood, undermines the presentation of Rust's pessimism as purely or even primarily rationalist, a fact that suggests fundamental problems for the project of seeing pessimism as a principled philosophy rather than an empirical worldview. This picture of pessimism as more personal than philosophical and more subjective than objective, more empirical than rational, seems to be confirmed in the season finale, where it is the experience of Sophia's love, a metaphorical return from the damage and suffering of her death, that leads Rust back to optimism. Because this is how the show ends, the question of whether pessimism is the result of philosophical reason or personal experience in *True Detective* might seem settled. And yet ...

"I Was a Part of Everything that I Ever Loved"

In the season finale, Rust has a near-death experience that leads him away from pessimism and back to optimism. Central to this event is his experience of Sophia's love:

> There was a moment, I know, when I was under in the dark. ... It was a vague awareness in the dark, and I could feel my definitions fading. And beneath that darkness, there was another kind ... it was deeper, warm, you know, like a substance. I could feel, man, and I knew, I knew my daughter waited for me there. So clear. I could feel her. ... It was like I was a part of everything that I ever loved, and

we were all … just fadin' out. And all I had to do was let go and I did. I said, "Darkness, yeah, yeah." And I disappeared. But I could still feel her love there, even more than before. Nothing. There was nothing but that love. Then I woke up.

In the darkness of his coma following his run-in with the Yellow King, Rust lies on the verge of death, his "definitions fading." In that darkness, he feels his daughter's love not in a partial or conditional way but completely and unconditionally: "there was nothing but that love." It is this experience that leads him back to the light of hope and optimism, the show ending with his proclamation that even though "the dark has a lot more territory," the fact that there is any light at all is proof that "the light is winning." One might see this finale as a selling out of Rust's pessimism, his surrender to optimism catering to a desire for a happy ending. On this reading, the season finale presents Rust's pessimism as ultimately more the result of personal experience than philosophical reason, the profound emphasis on "feeling" and "love" highlighting the pain and absence of love that gave rise to his pessimism from the start. Yet, when we remember the show's symbolic link between Sophia's name and philosophy, this conclusion seems problematic.

If, as the etymology of her name implies, Sophia is the figure of wisdom and philosophy in *True Detective*, then Rust's experience of her love at the end would be an experience of the unconditional "love of wisdom"—that is, an experience of pure philosophy or a pure philosophical experience. Rust's feeling of Sophia's love, on this reading, would not be a turning away from philosophy but a turning toward philosophy or perhaps a turning toward a different notion of philosophy than the one found in rationalism or empiricism. In this experience of pure philosophy, Rust both "knows" and "feel[s his] definitions fading," feeling a breakdown in the distinction between himself and the world but also a breakdown in the distinction between "feeling" and "knowing," reason and emotion, philosophical principle and personal perspective. In this experience of pure philosophy, all definitions and distinctions fade, merging into one another, philosophy being as much felt as thought, subjective as objective, optimistic as pessimistic. In this moment, the experience of philosophy would be the feeling of being, paradoxically, both a pessimist and an optimist at the same time. Hence, in this final scene, the show throws us a fantastic philosophical curveball.

Having led us to think the whole time that Rust's pessimism must be the result *either* of reason or emotion, philosophy or personal experience, logic or impulse, it turns out that philosophy appears to belong to both sides of this supposed opposition, a fact that would suggest that pessimism too is as much the result of reason as emotion, objective knowledge as personal experience, logic as impulse. Hence, in the end, pessimism in *True Detective* is properly on the side of philosophy, but in a totally different way from what the show had led us to believe, and in a way that challenges the attempt to make pessimism philosophical only by removing its personal, affective elements. And what if this is the real lesson of *True Detective*, and the real lesson of pessimism: that the meaningfulness of existence can always be doubted precisely because this doubt, this pessimism, does not belong solely to reason or affect, rationalism or empiricism, or principle or experience, since, in the end, pessimism will always lead us to doubt the very meaningfulness of this distinction? What if the real power of pessimism, like the real power of philosophy (and perhaps also the real power of love) is that it challenges us to rethink everything, to see, as Rust says at the end, that all of this—pessimism, philosophy, reason, affect, rationalism, and empiricism—are "all one story, the oldest, dark versus light?"

Notes

1. See, for example, Joshua Foa Dienstag, *Pessimism: Philosophy, Ethic, Spirit* (Princeton, NJ: Princeton University Press, 2006); David Peak, *The Spectacle of the Void* (USA: Schism, 2014); Stuart Sim, *A Philosophy of Pessimism* (London: Reaktion Books, 2015); and Eugene Thacker, *In The Dust of This Planet* (Winchester: Zero Books, 2011) and *Cosmic Pessimism* (Minneapolis: Univocal, 2015).
2. Thomas Ligotti, *The Conspiracy against the Human Race* (New York: Hippocampus Press, 2010), 43.
3. René Descartes, *Meditations on First Philosophy* (Indianapolis: Hackett, 1993).

5

Rust's Anti-natalism
The Moral Imperative to "Opt Out of a Raw Deal"

Chris Byron

The television universe of *True Detective* is quite bleak. That may be an understatement. It is often completely monstrous. The first season's two heroes and moral center are far from virtuous. Rust, for instance, recognizes himself as a "bad guy" whose redeeming trait is that he keeps "other bad men from the door." Most of the adult characters are either just as flawed or remarkably worse. Monsters such as Reverend Tuttle, Reggie Ledoux, and Errol Childress ought not to live so close together, nor be so institutionally well organized and socially interconnected. Philosophically, we should consider whether or not human existence in the world of *True Detective* is worth enduring.

Take, for instance, the children of *True Detective*. Although they are not categorically evil, they essentially have no real opportunities to flourish. They grow up in poverty and are spoon-fed a dogmatic religious education in schools filled with pedophiles and rapists. Although no individual child is depicted as evil, it is doubtful that any of them are going to grow up to be moral leaders and beacons of social progress. Ought the characters of *True Detective* to have children? Their children's prospects for success are dismal, and their prospects for abuse are too probable for comfort. Would it not be better if everyone in the *True Detective* universe ceased to procreate, and, as Rust argues in the "The Long Bright Dark,"

True Detective and Philosophy: A Deeper Kind of Darkness, First Edition.
Edited by Jacob Graham and Tom Sparrow.
© 2018 John Wiley & Sons Ltd. Published 2018 by John Wiley & Sons Ltd.

"walk hand in hand into extinction, one last midnight—brothers and sisters opting out of a raw deal?"

The philosophical position against procreation is known as anti-natalism, and no doubt Rust is an anti-natalist. Rust's insights, coupled with the philosophy of David Benatar, not only require the characters of *True Detective* to cease procreation but also morally compel all people to stop procreating. Indeed, *True Detective* creator Nic Pizzolatto acknowledges that Benatar's work was influential in the creation of the character of Rust.[1] Taking that cue, this chapter explores whether or not anti-natalism is a philosophically cogent position by presenting Rust's perspective on human existence and connecting it with Benatar's argument that coming into existence is necessarily harmful.

Rust Cohle as an Anti-natalist

In a deleted scene that initially aired in HBO's first showing of *True Detective*,[2] we find out that Rust's girlfriend Lori left him because he did not want to have kids. Rust says he will never have kids again and will not budge from his beliefs. Lori is insistent that Rust will not have kids because of "what happened" to him. She is no doubt referring to the death of his daughter. Moreover, she states that, no matter what reasons Rust provides, ultimately his anti-natalist views are emotionally driven by his daughter's death. Rust, however, insists that his anti-natalism is a "philosophical decision."

This is one of the few moments in the show when Rust does not offer a philosophical argument. Instead, he only offers his philosophical perspective. We know he does not want children, and he does not think anyone ought to have children, but he does not put forward his reasons when arguing with Lori. Yet Rust seems like a smart guy. He is philosophically literate, has an impressive stack of books in his apartment, and is usually capable of justifying and putting forward various arguments with reasonable conclusions. This discrepancy between Rust's intellect and his unarticulated argument for anti-natalism leaves us, the viewers, with a question: What are the reasons someone would be an anti-natalist, and is it a reasonable philosophical perspective? Moreover, is anti-natalism applicable just to the world of *True Detective* or does it apply to those of us who have lives that do not involve rapists, murderers, pedophiles, and cult worshipers?

Rust's Scattershot Philosophy of Anti-natalism

Although Rust provides no singular argument in favor of anti-natalism, over the course of the series he does provide several premises that could lend support to an anti-natalist conclusion. Rust is fairly confident that the horrors he and Marty uncover in the backwaters of Louisiana are not geographically unique. They are symptomatic of the fact that the world is "all one ghetto, man ... a giant gutter in outer space," as Rust says in "The Long Bright Dark." Given that the world is one giant gutter, Rust believes Louisiana has no monopoly on violence and human cruelty. As Rust states, "in philosophical terms" he is a pessimist. A pessimist believes that the bad aspects of our lives outweigh the good. While this perspective may sound morose, it is by no means vapid, and was first fully articulated by the German philosopher Arthur Schopenhauer (1788–1860).

In his essay "The Vanity of Existence," Schopenhauer points out the intolerable nature of the human condition.[3] We are born into infinite time and space but live for a finite time in a finite space. Our entire lives are spent trying to fulfill desires that nag at us constantly and only ever receive temporary satisfaction. For instance, hunger, thirst, and our sexual appetites are constant, and, no matter how much we quench them, they will nag at us for continued fulfillment. Moreover, the existence of all living beings on the planet is governed by a horrendous process in which some survive through the suffering and death of others. Consider how many animals have suffered for humans' continued existence, and then also consider how many animals have suffered for the continued existence of other animals. Such a consideration of nature affirms that the world is one big ghetto.

Rust's pessimism drives his view that some of our favorite institutions and beliefs are ultimately illusions. As Rust argues in "The Locked Room," the sense that one is a unified self with an identity, the practices of love and forgiveness, belief in salvation from sins, and the existence of a benevolent God are all contrivances invented by humanity in order "to get together, tell [ourselves] stories that violate every law of the universe just to get through the goddamn day."

One such story we tell ourselves is that having children, raising a family, and leaving a legacy are good things to do. But is this really true? Rust argues that the act of procreation is inherently selfish. In "Seeing Things," he tells detectives Gilbough and Papania to "think of the hubris it must take to yank a soul out of nonexistence into this ... meat, to force a life into this ... thresher. That's ... so my daughter, she spared me the sin of being a father." Rust's statement contains two implicit premises. One of them is a rearticulation of his previous claim that the world is one big ghetto and that the bad aspects of life outweigh the good. The second premise, though, goes further in supporting his anti-natalist perspective. He argues that an act of procreation is inherently hubristic: it takes excessive personal pride. Rust's anti-natalist argument seems to go like this:

1. Life is inherently harmful (especially once you leave childhood and become an adult).
2. Bringing a being into existence is inherently selfish.
3. It is not in any individual's interest to be brought into harm.
Conclusion: procreation is wrong.

We will return to premise (1) below in a broader discussion of Benatar's philosophy. But for now we should note that, if you deny (1), Rust thinks you are being delusional. Let's consider premise (2). Is it inherently selfish to bring a being into existence? Upon reflection, the answer is most assuredly yes. After all, until a being is brought into existence, it cannot have interests. All the possible beings that could come into existence cannot be said to have interests at all until they actually exist. Necessary conditions for having interests are being able to feel (particularly pleasure and pain) and being able have to goals and projects. Since beings that do not exist do not feel and plan, they cannot have interests. Thus, premise (2) seems safe. When parents desire a child, they are fulfilling their own desires and interests, and not the interests of the child, since the child, by not existing, cannot be said to have interests. But what about premise (3)?

On its face it appears true, but upon reflection it does not. Certainly none of us would affirm that we want to be harmed, full stop. And we spend a great deal of time avoiding pain and pursuing pleasure. But is it always in our interest not to be harmed? In one sense I harm myself when I exercise, because frankly it's tedious and painful. But overall I consider it in my interest to experience the harm, in order to reap the reward of health. Thus one could argue that a child does have an interest, once born, in being harmed, so long as it leads to an overall good life. Parents often punish children, but not always out of malice. One approach to parenting is to punish children, which is an immediate harm, in such a way that they grow up well-rounded and happy. For instance, Marty and Maggie are seen calmly punishing their daughter Maisie. They send Maisie to her room, and she is upset. However, over the course of the show, unlike every other denizen of the *True Detective* world, Maisie appears to grow up happy and well-rounded. If that is possible, then it is not clear that premise (3) is true. And, if premise (3) is false and we are unsure about (1), then, although Rust may be right about (2), it is not enough to secure the conclusion that anti-natalism is definitely prudent. No matter how selfish our procreation may initially be, if the child ends up happy, they may be able to state definitely in adulthood, "I am glad I was born" without contradiction. Note, though, that if (1) is true, the statement "I am glad I was born" is a delusion. So, while the initial act of having children is selfish, so far it does not follow that bringing kids into existence has to be bad overall.

Benatar on Anti-natalism

The philosopher David Benatar disagrees. In his book *Better Never to Have Been: The Harm of Coming into Existence*, he argues that bringing beings into existence is always a harm and thus that procreation is always wrong.[4] His argument rests on an asymmetry between the goodness and badness of pleasure and pain. By rearticulating his philosophy, we can see that Rust's anti-natalism is actually quite reasonable, and moreover that premises (1) and (3) above are quite defensible.

Benatar's first two points are that, generally speaking, (I) plea-sure is good and (II) pain is bad. However, it also is true that (III) "the absence of pain is good, even if that good is not enjoyed by anyone," whereas (IV) "the absence of pleasure is not bad unless there is somebody for whom this absence is a deprivation."[5] There is an asymmetry between goodness and badness with respect to the *absence* of pleasure and pain.

To justify this asymmetry, it is important to note that most people would agree with all four premises upon reflection. Take premise (III), which states that it is good when there exists no pain, even when no being is present to enjoy the absence of pain. We accept this premise concerning responsible parenthood. For instance, we think it is good that Rust did not get Maggie pregnant during their one-night stand, and it is good that Audrey did not get pregnant during her underage sexual escapades, because that would bring a harmed being into the world. If Rust, Maggie, and Audrey are going to have children, we consider it prudent for them to do so in situations where a child has greater potential for well-being and less risk of overt harm. This asymmetry between pain and pleasure is reflected in the sorts of procreative duties we expect from people. Consider the point this way: if Audrey were to tell us that she uses contraceptives because she is not ready to be a parent, we would consider this a good decision. We consider it good that she is fur-thering the absence of pain in the world by not bringing a suffering being into existence. Now, Catholics, for instance, may object to using contraceptives, but most still accept the premise in the form of natural family planning and agree that there are good and bad times to have children. The bad times are the ones when suffering is assured. We think people have a duty not to bring suffering into the world, but we do not usually think they have the inverse duty to bring happy people into the world. If Audrey never has a child, that is fine. If she does have a child in a reckless way, that is bad. Thus, an asymmetry exists.

Or consider another asymmetry. While we accept Rust's premise (2), that one cannot have a child for the child's sake, we do think we can avoid having a child for the sake of any future possible child. If Audrey, Maggie, and Marty all use protection when engaging in recreational sex, we accept that they are doing so to prevent bringing a harmed being into existence, and that is good (even if the illicit sex is not virtuous). Benatar summarizes this second point, saying, "It is strange to cite as a reason for having a child that that child will thereby be benefited. It is not similarly strange to cite as a reason for not having a child that that child will suffer."[6]

Another asymmetry in our moral duties is reflected in Rust's observation that he is happy that his daughter passed away before she could know true pain. Notice, however, that it would not be wrong if Rust had not brought a being into existence. We would not say that hypothetical being was deprived of happiness. We can feel bad for bringing a being into existence because it is harmed—hence Rust's claim that his daughter's early death spared him the sin of being a father. However, it would be nonsense if Rust were to feel remorse at not having brought a hypothetical happy person into existence, for the sake of that hypothetical person, since there is no one actually being deprived of happiness and pleasure. Although Rust could hypothetically feel bad for himself, he cannot feel bad for the nonexistent being.

Another moral observation can be used to motivate premise (III). When we finally get to see Errol Childress' home and occult temple, we know it is good when we see any area unoccupied by a suffering being. The emptier his temple and home, the better. The emptier Marty and Rust's interrogation room, the better. The emptier the backwaters of Louisiana, or the religious schools, or the entire universe of *True Detective*, the better! That is because the absence of pain is good, even when there is no one around to experience it (III), whereas the absence of pleasure is only bad when someone is deprived of it (IV). The only people it is bad to deprive of pleasure are those who actually exist—such as Maisie, Audrey, or Maggie.

We now have four different reasons for accepting the asymmetry between (III) and (IV). There is an asymmetry between our procreative duties. We should avoid bringing suffering people into existence but we have no counterobligation to bring happy people into existence. There is an asymmetry of beneficence in procreation. It seems too bizarre to cite a child's well-being as the reason for having a child, whereas it makes sense to accept the claim of possible parents that they are delaying the act of procreation because the future child will suffer. Then there is the asymmetry of retrospective beneficence. This asymmetry acknowledges the fact that, while we can feel bad for an existing child once it is brought into being, we cannot also feel bad for the children we have not brought into being. Finally, there is the asymmetry of suffering across space. While we think it good when an uninhabited space does not have suffering beings in it, we do not conversely think it bad that the same empty space does not have happy beings in it.[7] We do not think it is bad that Mars does not contain a happy civilization, but we do think it is good that no one is in Errol Childress' temple. Even if someone with a particular religious disposition rejects one of these premises, they most likely accept several of the others and thus support the overall asymmetry between pleasure and pain concerning existence and nonexistence.

Given that bringing a life into existence always constitutes a harm (since that life will inevitably suffer at various points), whereas the absence of existence is never a harm, it follows that nonexistence is preferable to existence. Coming into existence will always constitute some harm, whereas nonexistence can never be a harm, because things that never exist cannot be said to be harmed. Perhaps, then, Rust is right that the human species ought to opt out of existence, forgoing our mutual raw deal. The legitimacy of premises (I)–(IV) is just as applicable in the world of *True Detective* as it is in our own world.

Returning to Cohle's Life Is an Inherently Bad Proposition

Now, a person could read all this, recognize that procreation is wrong, and still decide that nevertheless they are going to procreate. After all, they say to themselves, life is not as bad as Rust states. This is a risky venture, since one is gambling with the well-being of someone else's life, and in any other circumstance we would find this sort of venture to be wholly reckless and immoral. Is Rust right, though, that most, if not all, lives are awful? From a historical perspective, the answer must be yes. History is one bloody and violent process where survival almost always means being able to kill another living being. Both the act of killing and being killed are frequently undesirable. Human existence is no different. The human species is at least 150,000 years old and, as the philosopher Thomas Hobbes (1588–1679) so eloquently stated, our lives have been mostly "nasty, brutish, and short."[8] Even today, a cursory glance through the morning paper reveals famine, inequality, natural disasters, terrorist attacks, psychological ailments, and the spread of disease, racism, sexism, and megalomaniacs running for presidency as if they have the population's interests at heart. How many people are really living lives that net more pleasure than pain? Even when our friends and family tell us they are doing well, are they not delusional, as Rust suggests?

Benatar cites dozens of studies suggesting that humans are bad at assessing how well things are really going and that they often lie when asked.[9] For instance, when someone asks, "How are you?" the knee-jerk response is "good." But oftentimes we are cranky, thirsty, achy, and so forth. Just as Schopenhauer points out, we are trapped in a perennial process of addressing desires, which, once satisfied, are quickly replaced by more unsatisfied desires. Think about all the times Marty tries to act as if everything is okay. Life is great, he is a family man, and has achieved the American dream. Behind all his smiles and boastful tales, though, we know he is unhappy. Aside from Rust, few people wear their misery on their sleeves. If this is the case, and happiness is a delusion, or something forever out of reach for the mass of humanity, then it must take real "hubris … to yank a soul out of nonexistence into this … meat, to force a life into this … thresher."

Notes

1. Michael Calia, "Writer Nic Pizzolatto on Thomas Ligotti and the Weird Secrets of 'True Detective,'" *Wall Street Journal*, February 2, 2014.
2. "True Detective Deleted Scene—Rust and Lori." *YouTube*, March 14, 2014. https://www.youtube.com/watch?v=89FObkqroZY.
3. Arthur Schopenhauer, *Essays and Aphorisms*, revised edition, trans. R. J. Hollingdale (London: Penguin, 1973).
4. David Benatar, *Better Never to Have Been: The Harm of Coming into Existence* (Oxford: Oxford University Press, 2008).

5. Ibid., 30.

6. David Benatar, "Still Better Never to Have Been: A Reply to (More of) My Critics," *Ethics* 17 (2013): 123.

7. Ibid.

8. Thomas Hobbes, *Leviathan* (London: Dent, 1947), 64.

9. Benatar, "Still Better Never to Have Been," 64–69.

Part II

"WE GET THE WORLD WE DESERVE"
Cruelty, Violence, Evil, and Justice

Where Is the Cruelty in *True Detective?*[1]

G. *Randolph Mayes*

Friedrich Nietzsche's (1844–1900) prophet Zarathustra famously declared that "man is the cruelest animal."[2] It's a nice tagline for a show such as *True Detective*, which entertains us with the fetishized torture, rape, and murder of lost young women.

To the extent that *True Detective* can be conceived as a dramatic exploration of human—all-too-human—cruelty, the crimes and their perpetrators are not of primary interest. I say this for two reasons. First, we are never provided with more than the illusion of understanding the crimes themselves. Does the cult behind them earnestly worship a bloodthirsty god who demands the sacrifice of lost young females as the price of its good will? Or is it a cynical alliance of social elites that uses religion as a front for enacting the profane fantasies of its members? There are, of course, suggestions of answers to these questions, but in the end almost everything about the brotherhood and its motives remains a mystery.

Second, even if we were provided with more satisfying answers to such questions, there is little in the show to justify the suggestion that cruelty is an essential attribute of human nature. A story such as this might have explored the idea, say, that we are all complicit in such crimes, that the cult is just a node at which desires and fantasies buried deep within the human psychosphere are actually enacted. Again, there are vague suggestions of this throughout,

True Detective and Philosophy: A Deeper Kind of Darkness, First Edition.
Edited by Jacob Graham and Tom Sparrow.
© 2018 John Wiley & Sons Ltd. Published 2018 by John Wiley & Sons Ltd.

but they mostly turn out to be red herrings. Not even the nihilistic philosopher-detective Rust Cohle seems to insist on anything quite so dark about Joe Shmoe.

So, where—if anywhere—does the interesting exploration of humanity's essential cruelty occur in *True Detective*? I suggest that it takes place mainly in the context of the most gripping aspect of the story, the relationship between the two principal agents. In a manner that is vaguely reminiscent of Apollo and Dionysus in Nietzsche's *Birth of Tragedy*, the struggle between detectives Rust Cohle and Marty Hart reveals a far richer range of human suffering and cruelty than the case they are investigating. And, importantly, whereas we are transfixed by the garish—indeed, nearly cartoonish—cruelties visited upon the victims, those that occur in the private lives of Cohle and Hart are surely closer to the reality of the human condition.

Knowing Cruelty

In *Thus Spoke Zarathustra*, Nietzsche wrote:

> O my animals are even you cruel? Did you want to watch my great pain as men do? For man is the cruelest animal. … At tragedies, bullfights, and crucifixions, he has so far felt best on earth. And when he invented hell for himself, behold, that was his heaven on earth.[3]

The idea that humans are the cruelest *animal* is interesting in itself because it implies that nonhuman animals can and do possess this disposition to some degree. This, of course, makes perfect sense in naturalistic terms. Humans are, after all, predators. Predators survive by killing and eating other animals. Killing typically involves the infliction of some suffering. Eating typically involves the derivation of some pleasure. Hence, if we think of cruelty simply—too simply, to be sure—as the capacity to derive pleasure from the suffering of others, it follows immediately that all predatory animals are cruel to some degree. Moreover, since humans are by far the most successful predator on the planet, it would be reasonable on this basis alone to claim that humans are the cruelest animal.

Nietzsche is in most ways a naturalistic thinker, but he does not appear to have had human predatory prowess in mind when he put these words in the mouth of Zarathustra. From Nietzsche's perspective, what makes humans the cruelest animals is not their surpassing ability to cause suffering and reap the nutritional benefits of doing so. Rather, it is that humans have developed a qualitatively distinct way of deriving pleasure from suffering. Not only do we derive all the animal pleasures associated with predation; we derive additional pleasure simply from *knowing* that we are causing another being to feel pain.

Of course there are primitive senses in which nonhuman animals can be said to know that another creature is suffering and to derive either pain or pleasure from such knowledge. Any creature that cares for its young, for example, will be sensitive to behavioral signs of distress that may originate in suffering. By the same token, any creature with a taste for blood will be stimulated by the sight of it. But it is widely agreed that most nonhuman animals do not possess what contemporary philosophers and psychologists call a "theory of mind." This is what gives almost all human beings over the age of five the ability to conceive of another being as having its own subjectivity, its own unique perspective on the world. When a human perceives that another creature is suffering, they have not simply observed the outward signals of distress but have also imagined *what it is like* to be that creature.

Embracing Suffering

But now there is something that seems to be not quite right. My knowledge that another being suffers just as I do, should, if anything, *interfere* with my ability to enjoy it. It should make me *less* cruel, not more. I taught my children to imagine how their mean and thoughtless actions are making others feel. This was not to introduce them to a novel pleasure but to make them feel guilt or shame and thereby behave more kindly.

Yes. That our theory of mind would be expected to inhibit our ability to cause other beings to suffer is an explanatory problem. But the real practical problem is that our predatory nature makes violence a necessity. If a theory of mind is to be useful to us—and it is enormously useful for predicting the behavior of other creatures—then it must not be permitted to inhibit us from satisfying our most basic needs.

Let's set aside the requirement of killing creatures for food and begin to make our way back to the show. As the foregoing example illustrates, parents wishing to correct their children's behavior must be willing to cause them to suffer. Among adults, our ability to maintain order depends on a willingness to enforce our laws with a system of punishment. The same applies to our institutions of teaching and learning. We encourage learning by rewarding it when it occurs and penalizing it when it does not. The same goes, of course, for the marketplace. The unproductive worker is cut loose, the productive one retained and promoted. Beyond the realm of deliberate behavior modification, an enormous number of human activities, such as the practice of medicine and athletic competition, entail the deliberate infliction of suffering. *True Detective* is replete with scenes in which Rust Cohle takes cruel satisfaction in explaining the sad state of humanity to his innocent partner Marty. It is easy to imagine a cutting-room floor littered with scenes in which Rust torments Marty with exactly this sort of evidence.

It would be fine to reply, as Marty in a lucid moment might, that in all such cases we deliberately cause suffering only in an effort to produce a greater state of well-being. The point would remain: we couldn't achieve these things if we were unable to knowingly cause the suffering of others. As noted, our capacity for contemplating the subjective experiences of others would typically inhibit us from doing so. The solution hit upon by nature was to give us the power to take genuine *pleasure* in knowing the suffering of another being.

This, of course, is Zarathustra's point about the invention of hell, which Nietzsche regarded as the ingenious creation of slave morality. The weak are only able to bear the cruel conditions of their own lives on earth because of the enormous pleasure they take in knowing that their oppressors will know infinite suffering in the afterlife. All of us experience the pure desire for evildoers to suffer, regardless of any future social benefit that may be thereby achieved. All of us also experience what the Germans call *Schadenfreude*—pleasure in the misfortune of others—even when the others are people we care deeply about.

To a large extent, our moral vocabulary seems built to hide our cruel natures from us. We do not typically say that we enjoy the suffering of others; we say they deserve it. Many of us subscribe to an unfalsifiable belief in karma, which permits us to simply assume that those who experience misfortune are being punished for past transgressions. Moral emotions shout down the guilt and sympathy we would otherwise feel when people suffer deservedly. Anger, resentment, and disgust seem to anesthetize us in this way while at the same time activating the pathways that provide us with genuine pleasure in their pain.

Clearly, our ability to enjoy suffering has enormous value. To the extent that it enables the judicious, purposeful teaching and training of the young, it has been an essential step toward the amazing fruits of human cooperation. Moreover, our ability to be cruel to *ourselves*, inflicting hardship and denying ourselves short-term pleasures for the sake of much larger but temporally remote rewards, is at the very core of human rationality. But this has also in some ways been a deal with the Devil. For the reality of human cruelty is that we now all have the capacity to revel in the suffering of innocents. To some extent, all of us feel the need for others to suffer, and, when we cannot find those who clearly deserve it, we *will* create them.

Although Nietzsche would agree that the ability to positively enjoy suffering is an essential step in the social evolution of human beings, it is not how he represents the ultimate value of human cruelty. Rather, for Nietzsche, the human capacity for cruelty is the key to affirming life itself. Nietzsche saw both Buddhism and Christianity as manifestations of the will to power of the weak. Having divined that life is suffering, Buddhism prescribed suffering's elimination through the extinction of desire. Christians, on the other hand, were only able to bear the torments of life on earth by creating an afterlife in which the faithful are rewarded with eternal bliss. In "The Locked Room," Rust ridicules this aspect of Christianity: "If the common good's gotta make up fairy tales, then it's not good for anyone."

Nietzsche saw both Buddhism and Christianity as decadent, as saying "no" to life, and as ultimately expressing a fundamental longing for death or extinction. Nietzsche even attributed this decadence to Socrates, interpreting his dying words—"Crito, we owe a cock to Asclepius"—as an expression of gratitude for his relief from life's torments.[4]

For Nietzsche, the key to affirming life was to categorically embrace all of the suffering that life entails. Nietzsche's model for this celebratory attitude toward suffering was ancient Greece. But he was, in my view, also fully aware that the human understanding of suffering has become far richer as a result of the increased sensitivity of human consciousness we see in the decadent traditions. Embracing the cruelty of the universe is consequently a far more significant and difficult act for a modern person than it was for a citizen of the ancient world. Yet it is precisely our developed capacity for delighting in the suffering of individuals that has prepared us for the ultimate affirmation of the cruelty of the universe itself.

Nietzsche's ultimate test of our ability to affirm human suffering is his doctrine of eternal return, to which Rust makes obscure reference on a number of occasions: "So death created time to grow the things that it would kill ... and you are reborn but into the same life that you've always been born into" ("The Secret Fate of All Life"). According to Nietzsche's doctrine, the universe repeats itself perfectly for all eternity. To the decadent, for whom the ultimate aim is release from earthly suffering, the eternal return is so horrifying a thought as to make you wish you were never born. But Nietzsche believed that the strong, who embrace all aspects of life, would embrace news of the eternal return as the weak receive news of eternal salvation.

Two Sufferers

The young Rust Cohle is no Nietzsche. Cohle's most consistent theme is the illusion of the self, which, according to Buddhism, provides everyone with a false sense of permanence and significance. In "The Long Bright Dark," Cohle characterizes human consciousness as a "tragic misstep in evolution" and embraces the decadence that Nietzsche attributes to Buddhism and Christianity when he informs Hart that the "honorable thing for our species to do is ... walk hand in hand into extinction."

In fact, however, Cohle has not come by his philosophy honestly. We are given every reason to believe that it is a view he has developed only subsequent to the tragic death of his young daughter and the consequent dissolution of a previously happy marriage. Neither has it provided him with any real peace or detachment. In fact, the cruel irony of his condition is that, while Cohle sneers at the throngs who participate in the illusion of permanence and the pointless suffering it entails, it is he who suffers the most. His knowledge has not given him peace; it has only made him angrier. He is angry that the illusion persists despite his awareness of it. He is angry that the throngs who participate in it do not understand how stupid and pointless their lives really are. Cohle needs others to suffer the way he does, and he is miserable that they do not. Hart summarizes Cohle's predicament succinctly in "The Locked Room" when he observes that "for a guy who sees no point in existence, you sure fret about it an awful lot."

Marty Hart is no philosopher, but he has a perspective on humanity that is not entirely at odds with Cohle's. Whereas Cohle seems to see the bulk of humanity as irremediably stupid and weak, Hart vacillates wildly between defending ordinary folks from Cohle's abuse and doing him one better. He insists in "The Locked Room" that without religion holding the threat of eternal damnation over our heads the world would be a "freak show of murder and debauchery." Where does this come from? Of course, he believes his job provides ample occasion to observe it on a day-to-day basis. But he clearly also detects it in himself. Unlike Cohle, Hart has suffered no great personal tragedy. He has a smart, beautiful, and dependable wife in Maggie, as well as two healthy and adorable daughters. He sincerely loves his family and desires to be a good husband and father, but he has almost no aptitude for domestic life. He is bored with conversation and lacks all subtlety and patience in dealing with family matters. His best memories of life with Maggie are the days before the children were born, when they would spend entire weekends in bed. As a young father, he feels unappreciated and sexually frustrated. Hart begins an affair with a younger woman, whom he treats as a toy. The affair will end catastrophically, and Hart, while despising himself for his weakness, will nevertheless feel that it is he who has been treated most cruelly.

Morally speaking, Cohle and Hart suffer in distinctly different ways. Cohle's professed nihilism about God and conventional morality would be expected to lead him to the view that "everything is permitted." But it doesn't. Cohle simply cannot use his intellect to escape the cruel tyranny of his character, which is that of a deeply responsible individual. Cohle is genuinely angered by Hart's infidelity. In one of the most powerful scenes of the series, Cohle mows Hart's lawn as a way to communicate the enormous risk he is taking by neglecting his wife and family. Cohle is fully aware of Maggie's attraction to him, but he has no intention of seducing her. When Cohle insists to a female drug dealer that "Of course I am dangerous. I'm police. I can do horrible things to people with impunity" ("Seeing Things"), we feel that he is trying to protect her from others, not himself. It is Cohle who, after 10 years of torturing himself in the cold of Alaska, returns to Louisiana because, as he explains to Marty, the two men "have a debt."

Hart suffers from the opposite problem. While he emphatically embraces an everyman morality, he is a slave to his basest impulses. Whereas Cohle would have passed Mischel's marshmallow test while still in diapers, it is not clear that Hart would pass it today.[5] Hart acts on genuine compassion when he gives an underage prostitute money to escape into a better life, but years later he can't resist when she returns to express her gratitude in the only way she knows how. After a decade, Hart still seethes with pure hatred for Cohle, though it was his own serial infidelities that resulted in the awful sexual encounter between Cohle and Maggie. Watching "The Secret Fate of All Life," we may chalk Hart's execution of Reggie Ledoux up to genuine moral outrage, but we eventually understand it as a reckless and selfish act that forced his partner to participate in an elaborate falsification of what occurred there. It also permitted the murders to continue for years after the case was spuriously resolved, with Cohle himself ultimately becoming a prime suspect.

Affirmation or Death

In Nietzsche's *Birth of Tragedy*, the spirit of Dionysus is represented as a raw vital force that, left to its own devices, is chaotic and destructive.[6] The Apollonian spirit, on the other hand, is the source of order and discipline, which, left to its own devices, is static and lifeless. Only together can they produce things of great, life-affirming beauty.

Though it is far from a perfect fit, we can see this dynamic playing out in the story, with Hart as the destructive source of Dionysian energy and Cohle as the tortured source of Apollonian form. During their decade-long separation, their lives lose all urgency and meaning. A lonely and dissipated Hart, estranged from his now ex-wife and daughters, spends his nights in a small apartment watching inane television shows and eating frozen dinners. Cohle passes time in Alaska as masochistically as possible, self-consciously destroying himself with drugs, tobacco, and alcohol. Both live in a state of Nietzschean decadence, repudiating their cruel pasts and thereby draining their presents of all value. Cohle's ultimate return to Louisiana is occasioned by his nagging conviction that there is unfinished business to attend to. He ostensibly refers to the crimes, but of equal importance is the unfinished business between the two men.

The young Rust Cohle was evidently familiar with Nietzsche's concept of the eternal return before Reggie Ledoux spoke of it shortly before his death. But in 2012, during his interview with Gilbough and Papania, Cohle, cryptically referring to Ledoux, says "someone once told me that time is a flat circle." He now elaborates the Nietzschean metaphysic with conviction. Throughout the interview, Cohle appears to subscribe to the pessimism he espoused in his earlier years. But I suggest that this, like much of what Hart and Cohle recount to the detectives about the events of 1995, is a ruse. Cohle is not the same philosopher he was then. Like Nietzsche, Cohle represents the eternal return to the investigating detectives as a horror, but he himself has come to see it as the one possibility of salvation. His purpose in returning is to discover a Nietzschean moment of ecstatic affirmation, one in which he and Hart might fully embrace all of the cruelties they have experienced and perpetrated. Or die trying.

Notes

1. An earlier version of this chapter originally appeared online at *The Critique*.

2. Friedrich Nietzsche, *Thus Spoke Zarathustra*, in *The Portable Nietzsche*, trans. Walter Kaufmann (New York: Penguin, 1982), 330.
3. Ibid.
4. Friedrich Nietzsche, *The Gay Science*, trans. Walter Kaufmann (New York: Vintage, 1974).
5. James Clear, "40 Years of Stanford Research Found that People with This One Quality Are More Likely to Succeed." http://jamesclear.com/delayed-gratification.
6. Friedrich Nietzsche, *The Birth of Tragedy* and *The Case of Wagner*, trans. Walter Kaufmann (New York: Vintage, 1967).

Nevermind

Subjective and Objective Violence in Vinci

Luke Howie

I live among you ... well disguised!

Vinci, California, is a violent place. Most would agree. But in what ways is it violent? What causes this violence? How do we know it when we see it? The murders? They're definitely violent. Velcoro assaulting the father of his son's bully? Yes, but so was the bullying. What about the prostitution and the live internet sex shows? Perhaps, but that's a little murky. What of the secret government and corporate deals? The pollution and poverty? Many would say these things are harmful but not violent.

Slovenian philosopher and psychoanalyst Slavoj Žižek believes that violent and traumatic events are indeed murky. If the violent story is too clear-cut, as in accounts rendered by journalists, then we become suspicious.[1] To clearly provide a narrative of one's experience of violence—if events are arranged in an order that is too consistent—suggests that the events weren't so traumatic after all. However, confusion, doubt, uncertainty, and ambivalence all seem to confirm that something terrible has happened that we cannot quite grasp. It is the "factual deficiencies," as Žižek describes them, that render something authentic. This is probably why art, poetry, and music have long been able to capture and communicate human tragedy and emotions that might otherwise be impossible

True Detective and Philosophy: A Deeper Kind of Darkness, First Edition.
Edited by Jacob Graham and Tom Sparrow.
© 2018 John Wiley & Sons Ltd. Published 2018 by John Wiley & Sons Ltd.

to understand or explain (and why Leonard Cohen's "Nevermind" really hits the spot).

Sigmund Freud (1856–1939) and his followers argued that violence and trauma take many forms. Žižek explains with a joke that makes a link between obvious violence and hidden violence. A man comes home from work early to find his wife in bed with another man. The wife shrieks, "Why have you come back early?" The husband responds, "What are you doing in bed with another man?" The wife replies, "I asked you a question first—don't try to squeeze out of it by changing the topic!"[2]

The lesson of this joke? We need to learn to change the subject! A lot of people don't want us to change the subject. There are powerful people in this world who want us simply to see what is in front of us and nothing more. When we witness terrorists open fire at a crowded party, do we also see the life of oppression that these people faced in the war-torn country where they grew up? Or do we simply dismiss them as evil wrongdoers who never took personal responsibility for their lot in life? When students shoot up their school, do we also see the systematic torture and bullying they were made to endure? Do we see the drug addiction, the mental illness, and a public health system that refuses to help the mentally sickest among us? And when we see corporate criminals, do we consider what it must have been like to grow up in a family where success was demanded and failure was worse than death? Žižek and season two of *True Detective* dare to ask these troubling questions.

"Subjective" and "Objective" Violence: Life in Vinci

"At the forefront of our minds," argues Žižek, are the "obvious signals of violence." There are murders, assaults, rapes, terrorism, wars, and torture. But we need to learn to "step back" and see another form of violence that lies beneath these most visible forms of violence.[3] A step back helps us to realize that these visible forms of violence would not be possible if there were not another, more damaging and deadly, form of violence that is so ordinary and everyday that we barely notice it occurring. Žižek argues that violence can be "subjective." Subjective violence confronts us on the television news with its often graphic coverage of wars, murders, assaults, and terrorism. Žižek argues that violence is more often "objective." When violence is objective it is less visible, operating *under the surface*, and is rarely, if ever, featured on the news. Objective violence can be found in the exploitation of workers in corporations, in the ownership structures of large media organizations, and in how societies are policed (think Black Lives Matter). Žižek breaks objective violence into two further categories—"symbolic" and "systemic." Symbolic violence is violence associated with language—verbal attacks and incitement and also relations of social domination that are revealed in words. But Žižek reserves his most controversial critique for systemic violence—or, as he defines it, "the often catastrophic consequences of the smooth functioning of our economic and political systems."[4] In plain language, it is ordinary capitalism that is the source of violence in society. It underpins the subjective violence we see on the news, and it is itself a form of violence. The second season of *True Detective* elegantly shows us why this is so.

*True Detectiv*e draws our attention to those moments when the violence we *see* is only a small part of the story, just the tip of the iceberg. The visible, subjective violence is a sign that there is a much deeper, much worse systemic violence at play. Žižek argues that any *system* that delivers prosperity to some and poverty to others is one that not only *creates* violence but is also, in itself, violent. Moreover, shouldn't we target the system that creates violence rather than simply treating the symptoms? Ignore the cause, and our symptoms return. Semyon, Velcoro, Bezzerides, and Woodrugh learn this the hard way.

Vinci is a city in decay. In episode two, "Night Finds You," Velcoro explains to Bezzerides how this happened as they drive into Vinci:

BEZZERIDES: What is this fucking place?
VELCORO: Suburban flight. Heavy manufacturing moves inland or overseas, plants close. Except here, a bunch of good capitalists ran in for cheap leases, tax incentives, immigrant labor, sweatshop economics.
BEZZERIDES: You don't have a problem with that?
VELCORO: No. My strong suspicion is that we get the world we deserve.

"We get the world we deserve" is a motif of the series and is featured on the cover of the DVD release. This is a horrible thought in a century that has given us 9/11, two international wars fought in its name, a global financial crisis (dubbed the "foreclosure crisis" in the United States), continued environmental degradation, peak oil, ISIS, and a host of seemingly never-ending disasters. Vinci is our capitalist nightmare! What makes it even more shocking is that it exists amid one of the world's most well-known and thriving metropolises. Vinci is not an abstraction or the mad invention of an overly imaginative Hollywood screenwriter. Vinci is Vernon, California.

The city of Vinci is a place where corruption, immorality, and violence are so commonplace that they are not only tolerated but also considered essential parts of life in this forgotten slice of humanity's seedy underbelly. Gangsters, prostitutes, drugs, crooked cops. Evil wins. The innocent suffer. Vinci is the dystopic vision of what we fear our cities will become. The horror of *True Detective* season two is that all this is already happening all around us. Vinci is a metaphor for all cities, a place where violence lives among us ... well disguised. The city of Vernon is a Southern California "corruption hotspot."[5] Vernon lies five miles south of Los Angeles and had a population of only 112 people at the 2010 census, making it the smallest incorporated city in California. But scandals have plagued Vernon:

- The city's founder, a Basque immigrant named John Leonis, ran the city like a feudal lord. He became mayor, issued business permits, and operated the bank. He was indicted eventually but not before amassing a fortune. During his indictment it was noted that he didn't even live in Vernon, preferring instead to live in a glamorous house in Hancock Park in central Los Angeles. The charges against Leonis were eventually dropped.
- Bizarrely, Leonis' grandson inherited not only his fortune but also the mayorship in Vernon. He too was indicted and accused of not living in Vernon, also preferring the affluence of Hancock Park.
- Between 2005 and 2011, the city was plunged into extraordinary debt. It was revealed that administrators had treated

themselves to first-class flights and $1,000-a-night hotel stays in New York and Ireland. The city's debt at that time was around $500 million.

- In 2008, a city administrator somehow earned $1.6 million. He later turned up dead in rocky waters in the Bay Area. His death was ultimately declared an accident.[6]

Sound familiar? Žižek likens this kind of dodgy capitalism to the old saying "you have to break some eggs to make an omelette." The problem is that capitalism breaks a lot of eggs but only makes really big omelettes that are consumed almost exclusively by the rich. As Žižek sees it, corruption thrives in capitalism, breeding people who want to "get an omelette without breaking any eggs."[7] Capitalism, in this view, is the embodiment of violence, the source of conflict, and the substance that organizes the world's evil. The "fate," Žižek argues, "of whole swathes of society and sometimes of whole countries can be decided by the speculative dance of Capital, which pursues its goal of profitability with a blessed indifference to how its movements will affect social reality."[8] Capitalism, it could be said, makes the world—and the people in it—vulnerable, *fragile*.

Frank Goes Straight

Frank Semyon is a gangster trying to go straight … well, sort of. He's trying to go about as straight as business gets in Vinci. Frank tries to make his money with the sorts of tax exemptions that Velcoro tells Bezzerides about on their car ride into Vinci. He wants to buy polluted land because it's cheap and comes with government subsidies. But such is the world of dodgy business. Frank is betrayed by the gangsters he trusts (go figure!), and the city administrator who was responsible for facilitating the land investment goes missing. He later turns up dead, as they say in the classics. The message? The whole system is fragile and can collapse at any moment. It's not made of anything strong or substantial. Frank comes to this conclusion while staring at his roof lying in bed with his wife, Jordan, in episode two, "Night Finds You": "How'd a water stain get there? It rained maybe twice this last year! It's like everything is papier-mâché!" In Žižek's psychoanalysis, the "stain" is an important idea. The "stain" is an intrusion into reality, a foreign and often unwelcome blot, a "splinter" in our vision.[9] In psychoanalysis, a stain can be a metaphor for a legacy, the prover- bial *making a mark on the world*. But the world makes a mark on us too. You might say that, metaphorically, the world stains our minds, and we in turn are stains on the world. The stain is thought of as the point when we realize we are part of the world we live in and the world is part of us too. It reminds us of our complex place in it. Or, to use the jargon, the stain is the "point from which the object itself returns the gaze."[10]

It is while staring at this stain that Frank realizes his world is brittle and threatening to come apart. It is all "papier-mâché." And it is the awfulness of his, and his city's, past that stains his life and the life of the characters in the show. Frank stares at this brown stain on his ceiling while lying in bed and tells his wife a harrowing tale from his childhood. When he was a child, his father would lock Frank in the basement while "he'd go on a bender." This would usually be for one night. Frank always assumed it was to keep him safe while his father was in no condition to look after him. On one occasion, however, he left Frank in the basement for five days. "By the second morning," Frank explains, "I was out of food." By the third day, the light bulb burned out, and Frank was left in complete darkness. That was when "the rats started coming out." Soon, he fell asleep and woke to discover that the rats had been chewing his finger:

> I grabbed it in the dark with my hands, I started smashing. And I just kept smashing it until it was nothing but goo in my hands. Two more days I was in there. In the dark. Until my dad comes home. ... Ever since, I wondered: what if he never comes home? What if I'm still in that basement in the dark? What if I died there? That's what that reminds me of. ... The water stain. Something's trying to tell me that it's all papier-mâché. Something's telling me to wake up, like ... like I'm not real. Like I'm only dreaming.

We learn that all of the main characters have harrowing pasts that are stained on their lives and their city. All of their worlds are a bit like papier-mâché. Bezzerides grew up in a hippie cult and was subject to horrific sexual abuse. She offers insight into her childhood when interrogating Dr. Pitlor in episode two:

BEZZERIDES: Five kids living there when I was growing up. Two are in jail now, two committed suicide. How's that for social theory?

DR. PITLOR: And the fifth?

BEZZERIDES: She became a detective.

Bezzerides. The spunky cop with the work ethic and questionable morals—she both abhors her sister's work in pornography yet engages in a workplace affair with a subordinate colleague, landing her in hot water with HR. The other characters have harrowing pasts too. Velcoro avenged his wife's rape by killing the man thought to have done it (with a little help from Semyon). The specter of whether his son is his own hangs darkly over everything he does. Woodrugh fought in a war and struggles with his homosexuality. In the first episode, he is falsely accused of bribing a pretty actress for sexual favors in exchange for looking the other way on a drunk-driving charge. This is particularly bad luck since Woodrugh is attracted to men. He finds himself caught between the shame he feels about his sexuality and the false accusations—he is immensely brave yet his greatest fear seems to be the idea of coming out. Bezzerides warns Velcoro of the dangers of these checkered histories in episode four, "Down Will Come," saying, "Those moments, they stare back at you. You don't remember them, they remember you. Turn around, there they are."

Through these characters, *True Detective* taps into the whole system of violence that characterizes the United States—the violence and criminality of international wars and the specter of 9/11 that made them possible; the history of social and sexual discrimination against people who are not heterosexual; violence against women, which is an ongoing story told throughout the series in relation to prostitution rings throughout Vinci and California; and industrial pollution and its shocking consequences for people and society. These are the stains that we all must live with. They stare back at us. After all, *we get the world we deserve.*

The World We Deserve vs. the World We Want

Which is better? The world we deserve, or the world we want? For Žižek, this world might be better described as a world we *think* we want.[11] Indeed, the world we fantasize about may not be a world we want to live in. You see, for Žižek, a fantasy must always remain a fantasy. The moment our fantasies begin to become real we realize they are horrific and terrifying. As long as they stay fantasies, they help us face each day. Would it be a better world if we were free to do whatever we want? A world that we can selfishly enjoy until somebody pulls our card? We all agreed a long time ago to live in groups, lest our lives be "nasty, brutish, and short."[12] We learned to compromise and build societies. We understood that we have needs but that so do others. Our needs can sometimes be satisfied, but we must be prepared to help others satisfy theirs. This arrangement has been formalized in the modern world. We call these arrangements societies or cities. But we can still have our fantasies—born of our desire—and dream of a world in other terms. And keeping our fantasies to ourselves does not mean that we can't get away with things sometimes. Sometimes our wildest fantasies seem possible.

In fact, anyone who even casually consults the media knows that powerful people get away with things all the time. When they do get busted, they seem to be able to explain what happened in such a way that we sometimes feel sorry for them. When powerful people seem human to us for the first time, we find we can relate to them. They made a mistake! Maybe they're not so unlike me after all. Transgression by the powerful "at the same time reaffirms the cohesion of the group."[13] Velcoro is aware of this, and, as their investigation starts to collect overwhelming evidence incriminating the powerful people of Vinci, he warns Bezzerides in "Down Will Come" that this will end with them in the firing line. Velcoro reminds Bezzerides that

> His [the mayor's] family's controlled this landfill for 100 years. And he lives in the biggest house on his street in Bel-Air. You think men like that exist without a long history of high-up friends? ... I'm gonna take a wild guess that you and Woodrugh ain't the most popular folks at your squads. Expendable, one might say.

Turns out the powerful can get away with a lot more than us ordinary folk. Indeed, as people operating across a whole host of social situations, we learn to do what's acceptable in those situations. A lot more is *acceptable* for those with incredible power. In psychoanalysis, this is called "repressive desublimation." It means that there are acceptable times to be as monstrous as we like.[14]

It is a world where the terrible things we do are not our fault. Not *really* anyway. We're only partly to blame. We can also blame our parents, you see. Or society. Or culture. Or maybe just television. Perhaps we can even blame capitalism, the root of all evil. In the documentary *The Pervert's Guide to Ideology*,[15] Žižek argues that popular culture is infused with the idea of the blameless criminal. He analyzes a scene in *West Side Story*, where a gang of toughs explains, through song, why they have turned out to be such social misfits. Žižek calls this "cynical ideology." We know we've messed up, abused our power, acted inappropriately. But hey, it's not our fault. Not *really*. Cynical ideology functions as "I know very well what I am doing, but I am still none the less doing it." The toughs in *West Side Story* sing their cynical story to the police officer who wants to arrest them. "Dear kindly Sergeant Krupke," they sing, "you gotta understand. It's just our bringin' up-ke that gets us out of hand. Our mothers all are junkies, our fathers all are drunks. Golly Moses, naturally we're punks!" The paradox, Žižek argues, is "how can you know all this and still do it?" We can answer this by posing another question. Who do the really powerful—and I mean the really, really powerful, like the Mayor of Vinci and his business associates—answer to?

"The Story's Told, with Facts and Lies ..."

For Žižek, there was a weird notion that swept the world in the latter half of the twentieth century that capitalism and democracy somehow went together. But this is probably not true. Capitalism is a better fit with authoritarianism. Žižek follows Karl Marx (1818–1883) in arguing that the twenty-first century is seeing the advancement of capitalism paired with its natural bedfellow. This coupling has, in reality, always been part of capitalism's story.

The task for us all? According to Žižek, we should not be treating the visible violence, the mere symptoms of an unjust society. Rather, we should try to build a society where subjective violence does not occur. And Bezzerides tries just this in the final moments of the season. Bezzerides mails the overwhelming case she has amassed against the powers that be in Vinci to the "authorities" … or whatever that stands for nowadays. She sends the package from her safe haven in South America. Her team is dead. She prepares for life in exile. Some justice. It is a moment for pessimism, perhaps. Žižek is not known for his positive outlook. The situation may indeed be hopeless—the powerful and corrupt win.

As Fyodor Dostoyevsky (1821–1881) told us in *Notes from Underground*, the story may be fiction, but the characters that are created must exist because the person who created the story lives in the world we have created for ourselves.[16] We should remember that Vinci might be *our* world—a place where the heinous violence we witness on the news is made possible by our unwillingness to confront those who benefit from inequality and greed. *True Detective* is a call for us all to do better as a society, as a community, as people. Will we hear this call?

Notes

1. Slavoj Žižek, *Violence: Six Sideways Reflections* (London: Profile Books, 2009), 4.
2. Ibid., 10.
3. Ibid., 1.
4. Ibid.
5. Abigail Tracy, "The Town in *True Detective* is Based on a Very Real Place with a Very Corrupt Past," *Forbes/Tech*, June 30, 2015. http://www.forbes.com/sites/abigailtracy/2015/06/30/the-town-in-true-detective-is-based-on-a-very-real-place-with-a-very-corrupt-past/″26011acc6195.
6. Hector Becerra and Ruben Vives, "*True Detective* Setting Based on California City with a Corrupt Past," *Los Angeles Times*, June 19, 2015. http://www.latimes.com/local/california/la-me-vernon-true-detective-20150619-story.html.
7. Slavoj Žižek, *Trouble in Paradise: From the End of History to the End of Capitalism* (London: Allen Lane, 2014), 30.

8. Slavoj Žižek, *Absolute Recoil: Towards a New Foundation of Dialectical Materialism* (London: Verso, 2014), 30.
9. Slavoj Žižek, *The Parallax View* (Cambridge: MIT Press, 2006), 17.
10. Ibid.
11. Slavoj Žižek, *The Metastases of Enjoyment: On Women and Causality* (London: Verso, 1994), 54.
12. Thomas Hobbes, *Leviathan* (London: Dent, 1947), 64.
13. Žižek, *Metastases*, 54.
14. Ibid., 16–17.
15. Slavoj Žižek and Sophie Fiennes, *The Pervert's Guide to Ideology* (New York: Zeitgeist Films, 2012).
16. Fyodor Dostoevsky, *Notes from Underground*, trans. Richard Pevear and Larissa Volokhonsky (New York: Vintage, 1994).

8

Naturalism, Evil, and the Moral Monster

The Evil Person in *True Detective*[1]

Peter Brian Barry

The theoretical commitments of Rust Cohle, the philosopher-detective of *True Detective*, tend toward nihilism. In the very first episode of *True Detective*, "The Long Bright Dark," Cohle explains to his partner, Marty Hart, that he is a "pessimist"—meaning "I'm bad at parties"—and a "realist." Cohle's realism is manifest in a tendency to avoid metaphysical extravagance. He has little use for religion, he repeatedly rejects the suggestion that the ghoulish crimes that he and Hart are tasked to investigate are occult or Satanic in nature, and his conception of human nature is sobering.

Bad at parties to be sure. In a memorable monologue in episode three of *True Detective*—from which its title, "The Locked Room," is drawn—Cohle contends that:

> All your life, all your love, all your hate, all your memory, all your pain—it was all the same thing. It was all the same dream, a dream that you had inside a locked room. A dream about being … a person. And like a lot of dreams, there's a monster at the end of it.

Just after Rust finishes his monologue and begins carving dolls out of aluminum cans, "The Locked Room" concludes with a long shot of the ominous Reggie Ledoux, the freakishly tattooed meth cook who makes cryptic statements about Carcosa, black stars, and eternal recurrence. Later, we learn of Ledoux's

True Detective and Philosophy: A Deeper Kind of Darkness, First Edition.
Edited by Jacob Graham and Tom Sparrow.
© 2018 John Wiley & Sons Ltd. Published 2018 by John Wiley & Sons Ltd.

complicity in crimes that strongly suggest that he is a moral monster. He certainly looks like one, although even he had a girl-friend at one point. Maybe there is someone for everyone in *True Detective*.

Cohle's remarks suggest a tenuous philosophical position. On the one hand, Cohle appears to be a tough-minded naturalist. There is no consensus about just what terms such as "naturalism" and "naturalist" mean, and different philosophers endorse different conceptions of each. Some naturalists insist that naturalism commits us to a certain kind of methodology in philosophical reasoning, while others suppose that naturalism commits us to supposing that everything that exists is natural in some interesting sense. But, if self-identified naturalists are united by anything, they are united in denying the existence of supernatural beings and entities. Insofar as Cohle dismisses talk of religion and demonology, he is pretty clearly a naturalist of some kind or other.

On the other hand, Cohle speaks freely about monsters, as is evident in the forgoing passage, and about evil. But, we are sometimes told, the concept of evil is "irredeemably religious or supernatural or mythological" with no home in a naturalistic framework.[2] As the philosopher Philip Cole explains:

> What we have here is a mythology of the evil enemy, such that the enemy possesses the demonic, supernatural powers needed to destroy our communities. This, surely, is a step too far—nobody seriously believes that migrants and terrorists have supernatural powers. But this is exactly what happens through the discourse of evil: the migrant and the terrorist, while they are not represented as agents of Satan, are represented as possessing demonic and supernatural powers.[3]

Cole is not alone. The complaint that there is something implausibly supernatural about talk of evil—say, because it is an archaic term intimately tied to religious discourse or at odds with a scientific worldview—is pretty common.[4] So, while it is probably true that few people really think that migrants and terrorists are super-beings with magical powers, it is also true that very many people use an allegedly supernatural concept pretty freely, as does the protagonist of *True Detective*.

If Cole (the philosopher) is correct in thinking that the concept of evil is at odds with naturalism, then it would seem that there is a problem for Cohle (the philosopher-detective). Should tough-minded naturalists like Cohle do away with talk of evil people? I want to suggest that the answer is "no." *True Detective* is a deep enough show that it offers some genuinely penetrating insights into evil and evil personhood. In what follows, I contend that those insights reveal that we can join with Cohle in endorsing naturalism without abandoning talk of evil people.

"Green-Eared Spaghetti Monsters"

If we learn one thing in *True Detective* it is this: evil people wear many masks, some of which make them look like monsters, some of which make them look like civic leaders. There are a number of plausible examples of evil people in *True Detective*: Reggie Ledoux might be evil, but so might the sanctimonious Reverend Billy Ray Tuttle, even if he's not so outwardly batshit crazy. But, if anyone in *True Detective* is evil, it is Errol William Childress: the "Lawn-mower Man" of *True Detective*, with a yen for torturing, raping, murdering, and ritualistically posing young women. Childress is described as a "green-eared spaghetti monster" by a victim who suffered at his hand as a child, and, while it's easy to dismiss this description as the sort of thing that a child would say, note that the creator of *True Detective*, Nic Pizzolatto, describes Childress as "a monster" and "tragically evil."[5]

Some philosophers suggest that there is a link between evil people and monsters: Dan Haybron intimates that evil people fall on a continuum between a human being and a nonhuman monster,[6] and I have suggested that evil people are moral monsters.[7] As is often the case in philosophy, a lot depends on just what we mean by the term in question, so we had better get clear just what we're talking about when we're talking about monsters. Understood in one way, talk of monsters is nonsense because there are no such things. Understood in another way, talk of monsters is fair game and perfectly consistent with naturalism. My hope is that getting clear about why talk of monsters is consistent with naturalism will help to show why talk of evil people is also consistent.

Stephen Asma contends that there are at least two prototypical qualities that characterize monsters: they are *unnatural* and they are *evil*.[8] The problem for Cohle, as noted, is palpable if they are both. If monsters are unnatural then it is hard to see how naturalism can allow that monsters walk among us. And if monsters are evil then we might have good reason to think that the concept of evil is also a supernatural concept alien to naturalism. After all, if evil is at home in the supernatural, why would it also find a home in naturalism?

But must we suppose that monsters are "unnatural" in a sense that is at odds with naturalism? Consider a very different question: Is a creature with an ox head and a human body a monster? That's pretty close to the Minotaur, the monster of Greek mythology killed by Theseus. Aristotle seems to think that, although such creatures "did not happen purposefully, but came about by accident," they are still possible given the laws of nature that govern the actual world and thus explicable by science, at least in principle.[9] By contrast, Noël Carroll defines a monster as "a being in violation of the natural order, where the perimeter of the natural order is determined by contemporary science"[10] and thus not the sort of thing that can be explained by science, not even in principle.

Given that Aristotle does and Carroll doesn't think that monsters are consistent with the laws of nature, Aristotle seems to be using "monster" in a *natural* sense while Carroll seems to be using "monster" in a *supernatural* sense. The prototypical monsters in the supernatural sense are vampires from Gothic horror novels and magical jinni from Islamic fairy tales. The existence of these creatures is surely inconsistent with naturalism. But monsters like the shark from *Jaws* are perfectly consistent with naturalism, as are Godzilla and Rodan and the Creature from the Black Lagoon. Aren't they just weirdly mutated beasties? Strange fruit fallen from the branches of the tree of life? There are no such critters in *True Detective*, of course, but they could in principle exist without violating any laws of nature.

Which sense of "monster" should interest us? It's not that one is right and the other is wrong, but Carroll's conception of a monster does have some odd consequences. In particular, if monsters must violate the natural order and cannot be explained by science, then lots of prototypical movie monsters aren't *really* monsters since their existence can, in principle, be explained by science—for example, Godzilla and Rodan. And that seems odd. So, while I don't want to say that we should disregard the supernatural sense of "monster," I do think that we probably need to hold onto the natural sense too. But, while Childress is surely not a monster in the supernatural sense of the term, he certainly can be understood as a monster in its natural sense. Moral monsters like *that* abound in *True Detective*.

To see this, note that Asma also observes that "the label of monster ... is usually reserved for a person whose actions have placed him outside the range of humanity."[11] What is it to be outside the range of humanity? Is it to be literally *inhuman*—that is, not a human being? Again, vampires and jinni are inhuman monsters in this sense, but not much else is. But someone might be thought to be outside the range of humanity in virtue of being, not literally inhuman, but *inhumane*—that is, lacking in the sentiment and sympathy that we expect from morally decent people. Childress is surely a monster given he is inhumane, if still biologically human. But regarding him as a monster for this reason doesn't commit us to believing in the existence of anything spooky or occult and requires only the natural sense of "monster." This is a result that should please a tough-minded naturalist such as Cohle.

Once we see that there are multiple senses of the term "monster" in play, we can easily countenance the existence of monsters consistent with naturalism. But we can similarly countenance the existence of evil people. Explaining why will require saying a bit more about the evil person.

"He's Worse than Anybody"

I've already suggested that someone might be regarded as a monster in virtue of being inhumane. But is being inhumane all that there is to being evil? Reasonable people might disagree here. Some pet owners and dentists are inhumane, but we might disagree about whether or not they are all evil. What's the difference between being a merely bad or flawed or nasty person and being a full-blown *evil* person?

I don't expect much argument that Childress isn't evil, but his seemingly mentally impaired sister-lover, Betty, suggests one reason for thinking that he is. There is a telling bit of dialogue in the final episode of *True Detective*'s first season, "Form and Void," and it's easy to miss. When it dawns on her that Hart is looking for her brother, Betty cautions that "he's gonna come for you" and "he's worse than anybody." That might not sound like much, but Betty's description of Childress aligns nicely with a thesis about evil people that I find plausible. According to this thesis, the evil person *just is the morally worst sort of person there is*. The idea is pretty simple: if someone is a bad guy but there is someone else who is still worse, then that bad guy just isn't evil. To put it another way: if someone really is evil, then there might be other people who are wicked or depraved in different ways and for different reasons, but there is no one who is a worse sort of person. So, if Childress really is worse than anybody, then he must be the worst sort of person and he is rightly regarded as evil.

I call this thesis, which I find plausible, the *modest proposal*.[12] Why modest? Because it is free from the metaphysical extravagance that Cohle abhors; it certainly doesn't demand thinking that there is anything supernatural about evil people. Nor does it imply that there is only *one* person rightly regarded as the worst in the world. Definite descriptions are supposed to pick out exactly one and only one thing: for example, "the present Queen of England" currently denotes exactly one individual, no more and no less. But some expressions that have a similar logical form will pick out multiple objects or entities: for example, "the tallest man in the room" might not have a unique object if there are two men in the room of identical height who tower over everyone else. If multiple people can be equally tall—or, for that matter, equally rich or equally qualified—why can't multiple people be picked out by the expression "the worst person in the world"?

The modest proposal is pretty thin gruel, to be sure, but it's a place to start if we want to make some headway in developing a naturalist conception of the evil person. To move things forward, focus on another suggestive bit of dialogue from *True Detective*. In the cleverly titled "Who Goes There," a despondent Hart probes Cohle with the following question: "Do you ever wonder if you're a bad man?" Cohle responds unflinchingly: "No. I don't wonder,

Marty. World needs bad men. We keep the other bad men from the door." This follows Cohle's earlier self-assessment: "I know who I am, and after all these years, there's a victory in that." By his own estimation, Cohle is a bad man. Hart seems to allow that he might be a bad man, and he's probably right given his hypocrisy, his endless moralizing about family paired with his continual cheating, and his willingness to abuse his authority. But, even if Cohle and Hart are bad men, they are morally redeemable to *some* extent; they are capable of heroic action and stand resolute in their cause. So, however bad Rust and Marty are, they are not the worst sort of person. Childress, by contrast, is an altogether different sort of person.

Now, most philosophers agree that being an evil person is *qualitatively worse* than being a bad person or even a very, very bad person. There is widespread agreement that evil people are not just *quantitatively* worse than merely bad people or even very, very bad people. It can't be that Childress, but not Cohle, is evil just because Childress seems to have killed more people than Cohle; that's a quantitative distinction. But it might have something to do with the fact that the actions that Childress is willing to perform are morally heinous in a way that Cohle's crimes aren't. Cohle does some bad stuff—and with impunity, by his own account—but he isn't a pederast and he isn't a child killer. That's a qualitative distinction. Similarly, it can't be that Childress, but not Cohle, is evil just because Childress is less sympathetic and compassionate; that too is a quantitative measure. But, while there is something morally redeemable about Cohle, there's nothing to be said on Childress' behalf; that too is a qualitative distinction.

Further, while we don't get much insight into the person of Childress, we get at least a peek behind the curtain. Exactly what he is up to is a bit of a mystery, but he clearly regards his mission as something cosmic. After declining Betty's invitation to sexual congress—"You haven't made flowers on me for maybe three weeks," easily the most twisted line in a series full of twisted dialogue—Childress explains: "Now Betty, I have very important work to do. My ascension removes me from the disc in the loop—I'm near final stage. Some mornings, I can see the infernal plane." What is he ascending to? It's not clear, but it doesn't sound very promising for the rest of us. That gets confirmed in Childress' longish, fractured monologue that he delivers in the epic final confrontation of *True Detective* as Cohle advances through a macabre garden:

> Come on inside, little priest. To your right, little priest. Take the bride's path. This is Carcosa. You know what they did to me? Hmm? What I will do to all the sons and daughters of man. You blessed Reggie, DeWall. Acolytes. Witnesses to my journey. Lovers. I am not ashamed. Come die with me, little priest.

What exactly does Childress plan on doing to the sons and daughters of man? He is pretty clearly committed to some grand, terrible project that is going to swallow the rest of us whole. His willingness to use and sacrifice other people is suggestive of a series of character flaws. On the one hand, Childress seems to suffer from the vice of cruelty to a pretty serious degree; how couldn't he, given his involvement with the murder of Dora Lange and the other nasty business taking place in and around Vermilion Parish? He surely suffers from other moral vices, too. His commitment to his project demands refraining from seriously considering how others will be affected. That is suggestive of a degree of moral callousness that goes well beyond mere indifference or thoughtlessness. In short, while we know little about him, we know that Childress suffers from some pretty grave character flaws. And this result is interesting for understanding what an evil person is like.

To be clear, it can't be the case that being evil is just a matter of suffering from moral vice. If it were, then Cohle and Hart would also be evil since they too suffer from moral vice. If evil people are the very worst sort of people, then there must be something qualitatively different about Childress in contrast to the heroes of *True Detective*. I suggest that the difference is this: Childress' vices are *extreme* in a way that the vices of Cohle and Hart are not. What is it for one person's vices to be more extreme? Vices can be extreme in at least two ways.[13] First, one vice can be more extreme than another given their comparative *intensity*: more intense vices are worse than less intense ones. This is a quantitative measure of extremity but one that seems to accurately characterize many putatively evil people: Adolf Hitler was not just somewhat unjust but very much so; Adolf Eichmann was not just somewhat callous but very much so; Ted Bundy was not just somewhat sadistic but very much so; and so forth. But vices can be extreme in a second way insofar as one vice can have *a morally worse state of affairs* as its object: vices with worse objects are worse than vices with comparatively better objects. For example, the objects of malevolence and rudeness are both morally bad but a state of affairs in which undeserving persons are harmed is worse than one in which they are offended. Thus, malevolence, but not rudeness, is plausibly regarded as being *extreme* in this second sense given that the object of malevolence is not just somewhat bad, but especially so. This is a qualitative measure; vices that are extreme in this second sense belong to an altogether different class of vices: the *morally worst vices*. The moral vices are most rightly regarded as extreme when they are extreme in both ways—that is, when they are among the very worst of the vices *and* possessed to great degrees.

Here is the basic idea: when we evaluate what sort of person someone is, we are making an evaluation of their character. So, the morally worst sort of person must have the morally worst sort of character, and that would seem to mean that the evil person must suffer from the morally worst sort of vices—that is, the extreme ones. But again, according to the modest proposal, the evil person *just is* the morally worst sort of person. Therefore, the evil person *just is* someone who suffers from extreme vices.[14]

How well does this result characterize the evil characters in *True Detective*? It really cannot be denied that Childress suffers from extreme vices, and again, this is a reason to suspect that he is qualitatively worse than the redeemable heroes of *True Detective*. But this characterization of the evil person is one that the thoroughgoing naturalist can live with.

"This World Is a Veil, and the Face You Wear Is Not Your Own"

Perhaps we are tempted to think that evil people must be monstrous to assure ourselves that, however much they resemble the rest of us on the surface, evil people differ at some deeper, fundamental level: they lack our basic human nature. And for that reason we can rest assured that we aren't like them and could never do what they do. But how much comfort is there in such a view? Is it really more comforting to think that humanoid monsters walk among us inflicting suffering and pain where they can? More comforting than allowing that real-life human beings might enjoy torture-porn and ritualistic murder? The supposition that our biology is a moral bulwark is a dangerous one in any case. Allowing that human beings can be monsters and that creatures like us can be evil amounts to acknowledging our corruptibility, and that is the first step toward preventing it. Anyone interested in combating and minimizing evil has good reason to share Cohle's tough-minded naturalism. Recognizing just what creatures like us can be and what we are capable of is one of the most important lessons of *True Detective*.

Notes

1. An early version of this chapter originally appeared online at *The Critique*.
2. Philip Cole, *The Myth of Evil* (Edinburgh: Edinburgh University Press, 2006), 18.
3. Ibid., 215.
4. Richard Bernstein, *The Abuse of Evil: The Corruption of Politics and Religion since 9/11* (Malden: Polity Press, 2005), 4; David Pocock, "Unruly Evil," in *The Anthropology of Evil*, ed. David Parkin (New York: Blackwell, 1985), 42–56; Susan Sontag, *Illness as Metaphor* (New York: Farrar, Straus, and Giroux, 1978), 85; Robert Wright, *The Moral Animal: Evolutionary Psychology and Everyday Life* (New York: Pantheon, 1994), 368.
5. "True Detective Season 1: Inside the Episode #8 (HBO)." *YouTube*, March 9, 2014. https://www.youtube.com/watch?v=cE2n-nwiqDs.
6. Daniel Haybron, "Moral Monsters and Saints," *The Monist* 85 (2002): 277.
7. Peter Brian Barry, "Moral Saints, Moral Monsters, and the Mirror Thesis," *American Philosophical Quarterly* 46 (2009).
8. Stephen T. Asma, *On Monsters: An Unnatural History of Our Worst Fears* (Oxford: Oxford University Press, 2009). 283.
9. Aristotle, *The Philosophy of Aristotle*, trans. J. L. Creed and A. E. Wardman (New York: Signet Classics, 2011), 239.

10. Noël Carroll, *The Philosophy of Horror; or, Paradoxes of the Heart* (New York: Routledge, 1990), 40.
11. Asma, *On Monsters*, 205.
12. Peter Brian Barry, *Evil and Moral Psychology* (New York: Routledge, 2012), 16.
13. Ibid., 59–60.
14. Ibid., 56.

9

"But I Do Have a Sense of Justice"

Law and Justice in the Bleak World of Vinci

Beau Mullen

The second season of *True Detective* has its feet planted firmly in the tradition of noir. Moral and administrative corruptions abound, allegiances are always shaky and uncertain, and the powerful are free to indulge in perversion and vice. The protagonists of the second season, particularly at its start, all appear to be acting to some degree in self-interest—rather than to correct an injustice—in trying to solve the homicide at the center of the story. The grim setting and violent, reprehensible actions on the part of protagonists and antagonists alike could lead one to the conclusion that, at least in the bleak worldview of the series, justice is not only indefinable but also ultimately unrealizable.

It is not surprising, then, that the narrative of the second season portrays the relationship between law (and codes of conduct generally) and justice cynically; law and its enforcement seem to be divorced from any conception of justice. Furthermore, the law seems to be primarily used as a tool for maintaining the status quo of exploitation. Given this cynical view of law and justice, it is equally unsurprising that we should find in the characters of Frank Semyon (a career criminal and ruthless killer) and Ray Velcoro (a substance-abusing corrupt police officer) an unusual exposition of virtue ethics and retributive justice. It is the conflict between these

True Detective and Philosophy: A Deeper Kind of Darkness, First Edition.
Edited by Jacob Graham and Tom Sparrow.
© 2018 John Wiley & Sons Ltd. Published 2018 by John Wiley & Sons Ltd.

spheres of justice that leads to the ultimate tragedy of the second season.

Law Divorced from Morality

The conception of the law as divorced from any kind of moral grounding is similar, but not identical, to the theory of law held by Austrian legal theorist Hans Kelsen (1881–1973). Not only did Kelsen see law as divorced from morality but he also saw justice itself as an irrational ideal.[1] Furthermore, he argued, due to this irrationality, justice is not something that can truly be known.

In contrast to the ideal of justice, law, according to Kelsen, is a specific form of social motivation and does not necessarily spring from morality or justice. Law is validated by being handed down by recognizable authority. Throughout the second season of *True Detective*, the viewer sees the law—be it the enforcement of actual codified law, the informal and corrupt order of Vinci, or the order imposed by organized crime—enforced to ensure that the individuals subject to it act in the manner prescribed by whomever holds authority. This is law at its most basic—social regulation to ensure domestic peace. The characters of *True Detective* largely obey whatever order is imposed upon them to avoid punishment, which Kelsen referred to as "sanction." Kelsen referred to this type of rationale for obeying the law as "indirect motivation," which he saw as the most effective method of social motivation.[2] Its inversion is "direct motivation," which relies on the individual to obey the law because its principles have been internalized.[3] The only coercion that is applied is psychological. Kelsen was highly skeptical of the effectiveness of direct motivation.

Central to Kelsen's theory of law are the concepts of delict and sanction. A delict is an unlawful act, the violation of a legal norm, and it is the antecedent of the sanction. In Kelsen's view, the delict is a wrongful act *solely* because the established legal order attaches a sanction to such behavior. Moral, ethical, and political concerns are irrelevant in this line of reasoning. Furthermore, in Kelsen's highly relativistic philosophy, roughly all legal orders are legitimate since they are all simply coercive orders that seek to regulate human behavior through the threat of sanction. The goal of such legal orders is social peace and limited violence.

Kelsen's jurisprudence explicitly refers to official norms, such as legal order imposed by the state. *True Detective*, though, deals largely with unofficial legal norms, such as those of a corrupt city and of criminal organizations. Still, the logic of an amoral order consisting of regulation through sanction of delicts is useful in coming to understand the culture of relativism in which our protagonists find themselves trapped. Ultimately, the protagonists of *True Detective* find the normative orders untenable. For example, Bezzerides, because of her romantic involvement with a co-worker (a delict, since it is against established departmental rules) is sanctioned with a demotion. This sanction is given despite her moral innocence. A more striking example is the murder of the informant prostitute Irina at the hands of the Mexican cartel members. When he discovers the woman's body, Semyon, who is himself no stranger to violence, questions why this was done. The reply from the smirking cartel member is brutally simple: she was killed for having spoken to a police officer—an obvious delict in the order of a criminal regime. Despite her transgression being minimal and causing the cartel no obvious complications, they saw fit to impose the most extreme of sanctions to maintain their imposition of order and to show Semyon, the target of their extortion, just how serious they are about maintaining their order.

The problem each of the systems presents to the protagonists, and hopefully the viewer, is that they are ultimately arbitrary and serve only those at the top of the power pyramid. The arbitrary nature of the orders, coupled with a lack of traceability to any formal norm, such as a written code or constitution (the existence of a chain of validity is also central to Kelsen's theory of law), results in diminished efficacy and violence. It is these relativistic and arbitrary orders that our protagonists rebel against, seeking instead to bring about solutions to the problems presented to them that are rooted in moral judgment and, ultimately, a sense of justice instead of blind adherence to an established order. Woodrugh, Bezzerides, and Velcoro disobey their higher-ups and effectively flee their power, and Semyon chooses to challenge those who hold power over him. All four, albeit to varying degrees, choose to make these potentially suicidal transgressions, acting in accordance with some moral code of conduct. In particular, a common motive among the protagonists is punishing those who have committed heinous crimes on the basis of the wrongness of the acts, not simply because they were a violation of a norm.

"Call It What You Want, Revenge, Justice ... Retirement Package"

A central conflict in *True Detective*'s second season is the tension between the impulse for revenge and the impulse for the more noble retributive justice. Revenge is typically based on an emotional response to a perceived wrong, and it aims for some cathartic relief or even the pleasure of the revenge seeker. Retribution, on the other hand, is based on the moral desert of those being proportionately punished and the idea that such punishment itself is a moral good. As legal scholar Michael Moore describes it, retributivism is "the view that we ought to punish offenders because and only because they deserve to be punished."[4]

Velcoro begins the season as a proponent of revenge—he kills the man whom he believes to be his wife's rapist. Yet, by the finale, the now changed Velcoro dissuades (initially) Lenny Osterman from taking his vengeance out on Holloway at the train station, convincing him instead that it would be better to see Holloway and his perpetrators exposed and presumably brought to justice through official means. Velcoro is in effect proposing to Lenny that, instead of the impassioned, violent (and ultimately self-destructive) revenge that Lenny has planned, the more appropriate course of action is one that exposes the culpability of the wrongful actors and makes them susceptible to the rebuke of society and the state.

A less perfect retribution is seen in Semyon's killing of Blake. It is imperfect first and foremost because Semyon himself is far from a legitimate actor: he is a criminal doling out punishment for an act—killing—that he himself has committed in the past. In fact, there is no empirical difference between his retributive act of punishment and the act he is punishing. He is punishing Blake's act of killing Stan by killing Blake. Second, Semyon has more than one motive for taking the life of Blake. In addition to punishing him for killing Semyon's subordinate Stan, Semyon has realized that Blake has betrayed him to Osip and his co-conspirators. Killing Blake serves the pragmatic purposes of removing Blake from the conspiracy and demonstrating to Semyon's remaining allies that he is still capable of decisive, ruthless action, not to mention deterring future betrayal. The line between revenge and retribution is also very blurry, given Semyon's apparent rage while interrogating Blake. Despite these considerations, Semyon's act could be characterized as retributive justice for two reasons: first, because the moral culpability of Blake is emphasized as the reason for the act of punishment and, second, because Semyon deliberately articulates his rebuke and wants to make sure that it is received by Blake. The fact that Blake receives and comprehends the rebuke is apparently just as important as his being punished.

Semyon could have easily sneaked up behind the unsuspecting Blake and shot him, had Nails dispatch him, or, more strategically, used him to deceive Osip. Instead, Semyon confronts Blake with the evidence of his misdeeds and interrogates him to find the last bits of information regarding his betrayals. Finally, as Blake lies bleeding to death at Semyon's feet, Semyon relates to him that he once believed that the young man had potential and that that was why he took the former fake-pill-pusher under his wing. This articulation finalizes Semyon's rebuke of Blake and communicates his ultimate disappointment.

Semyon's actions in this instance are in accordance with the model of retributivism put forth by German philosopher Georg Wilhelm Friedrich Hegel (1770–1831). Blake, as a member of Semyon's organization, which is itself a pseudo-polity with Semyon as its figurehead, is owed, as a member of this polity, the responsibility to be confronted and punished in a communicative manner. In Hegel's version of retributivism, the transgressor, as a rational being, has a *right* to be punished.[5] It is therefore wrong to deny him this right by not punishing his misdeeds. It should also be noted that Semyon takes no steps to hide the killing from his own wife, Jordan, which further indicates that he saw the killing as a justified act rather than a gangland slaying.

Some retributivists see the communicative and confrontational elements of punishment as its justification. Dan Markel addresses this in "What Might Retributive Justice Be? An Argument for the Confrontational Conception of Retributivism." It should be noted, however, that Markel's theory pertains to governmental actions in response to legal wrongdoings and would in no way condone or legitimate Semyon's action in practice or consequence. Markel writes:

> The action is undertaken in a way the *sender* of the message *thinks* will make sense to the recipient and is performed in a way that the thought conveyed can be made sense of, or effectuated, through the free will of the recipient. This communicative goal is realized even when the offender rejects the message, that is, he refuses to coordinate his actions or values in accordance with the message sent to him.[6]

Given the brutal and essentially lawless sphere that Semyon, Blake, and the other players in the action inhabit, it can be expected that such communication will take a violent, and final, form.

Finally, for all his amoral characteristics, Semyon also adheres to the retributivist principle that the guilty deserve and ought to be punished, but also that the innocent should not. For the most part, Semyon occupies the role of a sort of righteous bad guy—primarily harming other criminals and, further, only those who could be seen to "have it coming," so to speak. This is shown by his disdain when he realizes that the cartel has murdered Irina and regarding Blake's involvement in prostitution and human trafficking.

Semyon, however, is not above revenge. There is much to indicate that he himself cannot differentiate between justice and revenge. Take, for instance, the robbery of Osip and the slaughter of him and his men in the "Omega Station" finale. While convincing Velcoro to assist him, Semyon even states, "Call it justice, revenge … a retirement package." But the robbery is motivated primarily, if not entirely, by self-interest. Semyon and Velcoro need the money to escape and make new lives elsewhere, and they decide to take it from Osip and McCandless. Similarly, Semyon's killing of Osip is more certainly revenge than the killing of Blake. Semyon apparently derives personal satisfaction from the killing of Osip, and this is the primary motivation for taking his life.

While Velcoro and Semyon may have a sense of justice, it is certainly confused, convoluted, and even self-serving. The justice that they attempt to mete out is far from perfect. In *True Detective*, the blurring of the lines between revenge and retributive justice points to yet another philosophical point about the nature of justice—that its definition is maddeningly elusive and that it is often hard to tell when it has been done.

This paradox is hinted at throughout *True Detective*'s second season, especially in the finale. The protagonists make some attempts at immediate justice but seem to fall just short. Some of the corrupt apparatus is dismantled, some of the guilty are punished, and Woodrough is recognized publicly as a hero. The victories made by the righteous, however, are far from absolute and come at a very high price. The protagonists all experience great loss and most of them perish. There is, however, a hint that perhaps things will be made right eventually.

"I Don't Know if It'll Make Any Difference, but It Should, Because We Deserve a Better World"

Finally, the series' presentation of law and justice and the conflict between a retrograde system of justice that is the norm and a newer (for the denizens of Vinci) virtue ethic driven by moral reasoning is what brings about the inevitable tragedies of the finale—the violent deaths of Velcoro and Semyon, and the exile of Bezzerides. *True Detective* is, particularly in its finale, a good illustration of Hegel's vision of tragedy. In his *Aesthetics*, Hegel wrote of the nature of tragedy:

> The original essence of tragedy consists then in the fact that within such a conflict each of the opposed sides, if taken by itself, has justification, while on the other hand each can establish true and positive content of its own aim and character only by negating and damaging the equally justified power of the other.[7]

Velcoro and Semyon's respective demises illustrate this tragic sensibility; they are brought about by the collision of opposing spheres of justice. According to Hegel's aesthetic theory, tragedy is at its height when the spheres are "equally justified."[8] This is, admittedly, hard to say to the viewer about the opposing spheres presented in *True Detective*. However, that is most certainly not the case for the characters engaging in the tragic action—both were working against the orders that they had lived and worked under for presumably most of their lives. Both Velcoro and Semyon appeared to accept a barbaric ethic and conception of justice as a valid norm. Given the corrupt characters and culture presented by the series, it is only fitting that the characters bringing about the collision of the spheres of justice be as imperfect as the spheres themselves.

As Hegel scholar Mark W. Roche wrote in his brief explication of Hegelian tragedy, "Not only does the tragic hero refuse to acknowledge the validity of the other position, but the other position—or at least the sphere it represents—is also an aspect within the hero even as she denies it."[9] Both characters had lived and acted in spheres of justice (albeit skewed and ultimately illegitimate) that had well-understood expectations for the behavior of those operating in them. Velcoro was heavily immersed in Vinci's society of corrupt police officers and administrators and Semyon was an actor in organized crime. While certainly most readers would agree that the value systems at play in either culture certainly do not rise to the level of justice that each man dies aspiring to reach, these systems are not without their own value. They exist in their respective spheres to maintain order and to ensure that the dangerous actors operating in them do not turn on one another. Our protagonists violate these orders because they come to put other goods ahead of the maintenance of order and in so doing bring about much violence and their ultimate destruction.

This tragic vision is best seen in the fall of Ray Velcoro. Velcoro is of course doomed because he ultimately transgresses against the norm of his contemporaries on the Vinci police force. The supposed good of adherence to the norm is the preservation of order and the maintenance of the status quo. The maintenance of the status quo is ultimately self-serving for the local elites and the rule of law is merely a façade. Velcoro replaces his adherence to this norm with an ethic rooted in his devotion to his allies and his son. Velcoro goes from enforcing a normative order to actively trying to bring about its negation and destruction.

The death of Frank Semyon is equally tragic, although his ethics may be the murkier of those of the two characters. Semyon transgresses the order of the culture of organized crime out of devotion to his wife, to avenge the death of his subordinate, and to doggedly pursue what he considers to be his equitable stake in the empire he helped to create.

Holding absolute, unwavering positions and the willingness to fight, kill, and be killed in defense of the said moral position leads to death, if not of a tragic hero, certainly of somebody. For, Hegel, it is this conflict that ultimately brings about historical change. This can also be seen in the grim world of *True Detective*. It is no coincidence that the tragedies of the finale of *True Detective* season two are immediately followed by the implication that change may well be coming to Vinci. The last scenes involve Bezzerides talking to a reporter, giving him the information that could ultimately expose the culture of corruption and decadence that has ruled the city. What we witnessed in the bloodshed of the season finale was the violence of a paradigm shift, the old retrograde order attempting to quash the subversive ethic that is its polar opposite. While it appears that the status quo of Vinci has been maintained by the elites, the viewer is allowed to know that the subversive element is still very much alive as Jordan (Frank's widow) and Bezzerides actively work toward its overthrow and the establishment of a new, different order.

Justice and the Law

Despite being relentlessly grim, *True Detective* offers a valuable comment on the nature of justice and its relationship to the law. While the law may not be related to a code of justice, this does not mean that justice cannot be achieved. Despite the apparent victory of the antagonists at the end of season two, a hope for a just reckoning sometime in the future remains. Similarly, while justice is certainly difficult to define, particularly in situations where few are blameless, individuals can, through the use of reason, come to a working definition of the term and resolve to act accordingly.

Notes

1. Hans Kelsen, *General Theory of Law and State* (Cambridge, MA: Harvard University Press, 1945).
2. Ibid., 15.
3. Ibid., 19.
4. M. S. Moore, *Placing Blame: A Theory of Criminal Law* (Oxford: Oxford University Press, 1997), 153.
5. G. W. F. Hegel, *Elements of the Philosophy of Right*, ed. Allen W. Wood, trans. H. B. Nisbet (Cambridge: Cambridge University Press, 1991).

6. Dan Markel, "What Might Retributive Justice Be? An Argument for the Confrontational Conception of Retributivism," in *Retributivism: Essays on Theory and Policy*, ed. Mark D. White (Oxford: Oxford University Press, 2011), 49.
7. Cited in Mark W. Roche, "Introduction to Hegel's Theory of Tragedy," *PhaenEx* 1, no. 2 (2006), 12.
8. Ibid.
9. Ibid., 14.

Part III

"EVERYBODY'S NOBODY"
Consciousness, Existence, and Identity

A Dream Inside a Locked Room

The Illusion of Self[1]

Evan Thompson

In the third episode of season one of *True Detective*, "The Locked Room," detective Rust Cohle explains that your life, all your subjective experiences, are "a dream … inside a locked room, a dream about being a person." In his view, we are creatures who "labor under the illusion of having a self." These ideas—that all of life is a dream, that we might think we're awake when we're really dreaming, and that the self is an illusion—are some of humanity's oldest and most enduring philosophical thoughts, in both Eastern and Western traditions. So, too, is the question of whether transcendence—deliverance or awakening from the dream—is possible, especially at the moment of death. This question consumes Cohle and is a driving question of the whole of the first season of *True Detective*.

Life Is a Dream

In "The Locked Room," Cohle tells the two police officers interviewing him that when you look into a dead body's eyes—even in a picture—you see "an unmistakable relief." You can tell that the person, having been afraid, saw, "for the very first time, how easy it was to just let go." Cohle links this realization about death to the realization that life is a dream: "In that last nanosecond, they saw

True Detective and Philosophy: A Deeper Kind of Darkness, First Edition.
Edited by Jacob Graham and Tom Sparrow.

what they were—that you, yourself … all your life … was all the same dream, a dream that you had inside a locked room, a dream about being a person."

Cohle tells his partner, Marty Hart, in "The Long Bright Dark," that "we labor under the illusion of having a self." Death releases us from the labor and ends the dream. Yet Cohle seems ambivalent. On the one hand, he says that, in the last moment, you can let go and realize your life was a dream—the implication being that death delivers us from the dream. On the other hand, he ends his musings to the two detectives by saying, "And like a lot of dreams, there's a monster at the end of it." So, at the end, are we delivered from the dream or does the dream turn into a nightmare?

This worry encapsulates Cohle's ambivalence about human life. His existential predicament is that he's driven to seek transcendence—deliverance from illusion—yet all the while he denies or doubts that transcendence exists. This predicament makes him not just a "pessimist" (as he describes himself) but also a "nihilist"—someone who denies that life has meaning (because meaning could come only from transcendence) but who can't help yearning and searching for it anyway.

I'll come back to nihilism later. First I want to talk about Cohle's statement that life is a dream about being a person.

Eastern Views

The idea that life might be a dream, and hence that the world you perceive and the self you seem to be or have aren't real, is one of humanity's oldest and most enduring philosophical thoughts. So, too, is the idea that, if life is a dream, death might bring deliverance from it, either by being a peaceful state like deep sleep, undisturbed by any dream, or by being a kind of higher or greater awakening. (These ideas are central themes of my book *Waking, Dreaming, Being*.[2])

The oldest versions of these ideas come from Indian philosophy. In the *Upanishads*, ancient Indian scriptures dating back to the seventh century BCE, the whole of sentient existence—which includes not just this life but also a beginningless series of previous lives and an endless succession of future ones—is like being in one big locked room, in which we dream, over and over again, of being a person (a different person for each life). We think we're free, but we're really chained to an endless cycle of misidentification with a series of illusory, dreamed characters. Liberation, true freedom, comes from waking up from this otherwise never-ending dream. Awakening and release, however, can happen only when we realize through deep meditation that our self as it appears to us in both waking life and the dream state is unreal, and that our true self (*ātman*) is pure, cosmic being (*brahman*). Attaining this realization provides freedom at death, so that there is no longer the dream of being a person—of being a limited self—but instead the blissful experience of oneness and unlimited being.

A thousand years later, the Hindu philosophers, Gauḍapāda (ca. eighth century CE) and Śaṅkara (788–820 CE), who inaugurated the Advaita Vedānta school, systematized these ideas in their philosophical commentaries on the *Upanishads*. They argued that the self and the world as they appear in the waking state are illusions produced by the mind, a false reality like what we see in a dream. The individual self is an ignorant, mental superimposition onto the one universal consciousness, which is no different from pure being and limitless bliss.

A different version—still from India—of the idea that the self is an illusion comes from the Buddhist philosopher Vasubandhu (fourth to fifth centuries CE). In his view, unlike that of the Vedāntins, there is no true self in the form of universal consciousness; there are only innumerably many distinct streams of awareness, each of which is "empty" of a self—that is, empty of anything that would "own" the awareness and be the thinker of thoughts and the doer of deeds. Analyzing each mental stream reveals that it's really just a series of impersonal, transitory, and discrete moments of awareness, with each prior moment related to the next one as cause to effect. The illusion of self arises from the feeling of there being an "I" present at each moment and of its being the same "I" from one moment to the next. In reality, however, no "I" or owner is present at any point, so the impression of self is an illusion.

Vasubandhu also argued that the perceptual world is like a dream or a magician's illusion, because it doesn't exist in the way that it appears to exist. It appears to exist as an independent, physical world, but it's really just a projection of the mental stream. Like a dream, it has no reality independent of the mind. Moreover, there's no self behind the scenes responsible for the projection; there's only the cause–effect series of dependent, mental events, which produce the illusion of a self as a result of ignorance and attachment to the "I" feeling. Enlightenment or awakening requires seeing through the illusion of an independent self and an independent world, and eliminating all attachment to it.

In ancient China, the philosopher Zhuang Zhou (369–286 BCE ...) also likened life to a dream. In his famous parable known as "The Butterfly Dream," he wrote:

> Once Zhuang Zhou dreamt he was a butterfly, fluttering about joyfully just as a butterfly would. He followed his whims exactly as he liked and knew nothing about Zhuang Zhou. Suddenly he awoke, and there he was, the startled Zhuang Zhou in the flesh. He did not know if Zhou had been dreaming he was a butterfly, or if a butterfly was now dreaming it was Zhou. Surely, Zhou and a butterfly count as two distinct identities! Such is what we call the transformation of one thing into another.[3]

In this parable, there is an undecidable alternation between being a butterfly and being a person, with each phase being equally awake and dreaming. The traditional interpretation of this parable relates it to life and death. Guo Xiang (252–312 CE), the first and most important commentator on Zhuang Zhou, put it this way: "The distinction between dreaming and waking is no different from the differentiation, the debate, between life and death."[4] Dreaming is no less real than waking; death is no less real than life. The "transformation of one thing into another" includes waking and dreaming, as well as life and death.

Zhuang Zhou also wrote about what he called the "great awakening": "Perhaps a great awakening would reveal all of this to be a vast dream. And yet, fools imagine they are already awake—how clearly and certainly they understand it all!"[5]

Western Views

In Western philosophy, the thought that life could be a dream is linked not so much to reflections on life, death, and transcendence as it is to the problem of whether it's possible to have certain knowledge (a problem known as "philosophical skepticism"). For example, in Plato's (428–348 BCE) dialogue *Theaetetus*, Socrates asks the young mathematician Theaetetus what evidence he could have to prove either that they're awake and talking to each other or that they're asleep and all their thoughts are a dream. Theaetetus admits he doesn't know how to prove the one any more than the other, for the two states seem to match; even dreaming that you're telling someone a dream seems strangely similar to really telling someone a dream. "So you see," Socrates concludes, "it is disputable even whether we are awake or asleep."[6]

Two thousand years later, René Descartes (1596–1650) asked the same question in his *Meditations on First Philosophy*, where he argued that there are no "sure signs" to differentiate with complete certainty waking-sense experiences from dream experiences.[7] Any sign you point to—for example, sensory vividness—could also be present in a dream.

One way to draw together these Eastern and Western philosophical threads is with the following line of thought, taken from Wendy Doniger's classic book on Indian and Western views of dreaming, *Dreams, Illusion, and Other Realities*.[8] We can verify the hypothesis that we're dreaming by waking up—either from the dream (normal waking) or within the dream (lucid dreaming). And (what amounts to the same thing) we can falsify the hypothesis that we're awake by waking up—again either from the dream or within the dream. But we can't falsify the hypothesis that we're dreaming or (what amounts to the same thing) verify the hypothesis that we're awake. The reason is that for any experience we choose—specifically, any experience we take to be a waking one—it seems conceivable that we could wake up from that experience (remember Zhuang Zhou's "great awakening").

Modern brain science puts a new twist on the idea that life is like a dream and the self is an illusion. In the 1990s, neuroscientists Rodolfo Llinás and Denis Paré proposed that our consciousness presents us with a model of the world constructed by the brain. When we're awake, the model relies more on external, sensory information, and when we're asleep and dreaming it relies more on memories and expectations. The model in the two states is basically the same; it's only the main information source that differs. For this reason, Llinás and Paré described dreaming as a special case of perception without external sensory input and perception as a special case of dreaming with external sensory input. In Llinás' words: "Comforting or disturbing, the fact is that we are basically dreaming machines that construct virtual models of the world."[9]

"Neurophilosopher" Thomas Metzinger applies this idea to the self. He argues that the brain generates its own internal model of the world and includes in the model a self that knows this world. In this way, the brain is always "dreaming at the world," including dreaming that it is or has a self. The principal difference between wakefulness and dreaming is that the brain's activity has closer ties to sensory and motor information from the outside world in wakefulness than it does in dreaming. Nevertheless, in both cases, the brain generates an image of a real, independent self, but in reality there is no self; there's only the brain's model of a self. In Metzinger's words, "no such things as selves exist in the world: Nobody ever had or was a self. ... All that ever existed were conscious self-models that could not be recognized as models."[10]

Cohle seems to have read Metzinger, because he states this viewpoint to Hart in the first episode: "We are things that labor under the illusion of having a self. This accretion of sensory experience and feeling, programmed with total assurance that we are each somebody, when in fact everybody is nobody."

Pessimism and Nihilism

Cohle says that he is, in philosophical terms, a "pessimist." As several others explain in their chapters in this volume, pessimism is associated with the philosophy of Arthur Schopenhauer (1788–1860). Schopenhauer was influenced by early, inaccurate European translations of Indian philosophical texts, and he misunderstood Buddhism and Hinduism as pessimistic religions, ones that believe human existence is inherently unsatisfactory and that the best thing for humans is not to exist (whereas, on the contrary, both religions assert that human existence provides a precious opportunity for true awakening or enlightenment, and both uphold the value of selfless love). Cohle, at the outset of the story, subscribes to these pessimistic beliefs. As he says to Hart:

> I believe human consciousness is a tragic misstep in evolution. We became too self-aware. Nature created an aspect of nature separate

from itself; we are creatures that should not exist by natural law. ...
I think the honorable thing for our species to do is deny our programming, stop reproducing. Walk hand in hand into extinction,
one last midnight—brothers and sisters opting out of a raw deal.

Although Cohle is right that these beliefs make him a pessimist,
he's better described as a "nihilist" in the sense that Friedrich Nietzsche (1844–1900) gave to this term and that he used to describe
Schopenhauer. Nietzsche wrote:

> A nihilist is a man who judges of the world as it is that it ought *not* to
> be, and of the world as it ought to be that it does not exist. According
> to this view, our existence (action, suffering, willing, feeling) has no
> meaning.[11]

This statement captures Cohle's beliefs: the world as it is with
human consciousness ought not to exist, and the world as it ought
to be—either minus human existence or with real meaning and
transcendence—does not exist. When Hart asks "What's the point
of getting out of bed in the morning?" Cohle answers, "I tell myself
I bear witness, but the real answer is that it's obviously my programming, and I lack the constitution for suicide." This is the
nihilist's predicament—being incapable of giving up on meaning
(what's the point of bearing witness if there's no meaning?) and
continuing to experience things (such as the self) as having a reality that one believes or senses is an illusion.

  Nihilism, in this philosophical sense, comes from a deep insight
gone awry. The insight is that things do not have the kind of being
or reality that they seem to have. They seem to have their own
intrinsic and independent being, but upon analysis they turn out
to be relational and interdependent. There seems to be an independent "I," with its own intrinsic identity, but upon analysis there
turns out to be only a constantly changing web of interdependent
physical and mental processes that make up what we think of as a
person. Where this insight goes awry, however, is in the inference
that nothing has any meaning and that everybody is nobody. The
mistake is to suppose that, if there were meaning, it would have
to be grounded in something that has intrinsic and independent
being—such as God or the self or the soul. In this way, the nihilist
accepts the absolutist's premise about what meaning is, but then,

upon realizing that this kind of intrinsic being is nowhere to be found, mistakenly concludes that there is no meaning. In the case of the self, the nihilist accepts the premise that, if there were a self, it would have to be an independent thing or entity (a "substance," in philosophical terms) and then, upon realizing that this kind of self is nowhere to be found, mistakenly concludes that there is no self in any sense and that everybody is nobody.

In *Waking, Dreaming, Being*, I call this viewpoint "neuro-nihilism." The neuro-nihilist says that our brain creates the illusion of self and that we can't help but labor under the illusion, because that's the way our brain is designed. I argue against neuro-nihilism. Although I agree that there's no ready-made thing or entity or substance that is the self, and that our sense of self is a biological, psychological, and social construction, it doesn't follow that it's nothing but an illusion and that everybody is nobody. The self isn't a thing; it's a process—one that enacts an "I" and in which the "I" is no different from the process itself, rather like the way dancing is a process that enacts a dance and in which the dance is no different from the dancing. From this "enactive" perspective, although meaning and the self have no absolute foundation, neither are they complete illusions or nonexistent; they're brought forth in how we act and live our lives.

Transcendence

In the last episode of season one, Cohle, in the hospital after having almost been killed, tells Hart about his experience of nearly dying. The story comes back to the question—the driving one of the whole drama—of whether, at the end, as we realize life is a dream, we're delivered from the dream or it turns into a nightmare with a monster waiting for us. What Cohle earlier saw in the dead victims' eyes—"how easy it was to just let go"—happened to him. Reduced to a "vague awareness in the dark," his "definitions fading," he feels another deeper and warmer darkness, permeated by love and the presence of his dead daughter and father. He lets go into the darkness, affirms it, and feels nothing but love. And then he wakes up. Transcendence—of the dream of being a person, of laboring under the illusion of self—is possible after all and comes from selfless love.

Notes

1. An earlier version of this chapter originally appeared online at *The Critique*.
2. Evan Thompson, *Waking, Dreaming, Being: Self and Consciousness in Neuroscience, Meditation, and Philosophy* (New York: Columbia University Press, 2015).
3. Brook Ziporyn, trans., *Zhuangzi: The Essential Writings* (Indianapolis: Hackett, 2009), 21.
4. Ibid., 262.
5. Ibid., 19.
6. Plato, *Theaetetus*, in *Theaetetus and Sophist*, trans. Harold North Fowler (Cambridge, MA: Loeb Classical Library, 1921), 158c–d.
7. René Descartes, *Meditations on First Philosophy*, second edition, trans. and ed. John Cottingham (Cambridge: Cambridge University Press, 2017), 16.
8. Wendy Doniger, *Dreams, Illusion and Other Realities* (Chicago: University of Chicago Press, 1984), 37–52, 175–205; see also my *Waking, Dreaming, Being*, 94.
9. Rodolfo Llinás, *I of the Vortex: From Neurons to Self* (Cambridge, MA: MIT Press, 2001), 94.
10. Thomas Metzinger, *Being No One: The Self-Model Theory of Subjectivity* (Cambridge, MA: MIT Press, 2003), 1.
11. Friedrich Nietzsche, *The Will to Power*, trans. Walter Kaufmann and R. J. Hollingdale, ed. Walter Kaufmann (New York: Vintage, 1968), 318.

I Am Not Who I Used to Be, But Am I Me?

Personal Identity and the Narrative of Rust

Andrew M. Winters

For by one Spirit, we were all baptized into one body. ... For the body is not one member, but many.
—1 Corinthians 12:13–14

Who are you? This question is simply phrased but difficult to answer. It is an accomplishment to know who you are. As Rustin Cohle puts it in the second episode of the first season of *True Detective*, "I know who I am, and ... there's a victory in that." Here's why knowing who you are is a victory.

You are not the same person you used to be. This claim is obvious. You have aged, your body has gone through changes, you have more achievements, you know different facts, you have different ideas, and you have different social relations. Even in the past twenty-four hours, you have undergone various phases of hunger, fatigue, and arousal. All of this indicates that you are a different person from who you used to be.

Despite being a different person from who you were even just a few minutes ago, there is something oddly familiar about the person you no longer are. You know that person better than anyone else due to the range of characteristics, experiences, and memories you share. Yet, you are no longer that person. We know that you

True Detective and Philosophy: A Deeper Kind of Darkness, First Edition.
Edited by Jacob Graham and Tom Sparrow.
© 2018 John Wiley & Sons Ltd. Published 2018 by John Wiley & Sons Ltd.

are no longer that person because *that person* no longer exists, whereas *you* do exist.

So the questions remain: Who are you? What are you? In addition to these lingering questions, there are others that highlight some of the reasons it is a "victory" when you know who you are. These questions include: How can you be so familiar with something that does not exist? How does the person you used to be make you who you presently are? In this chapter, we'll explore these questions while considering how the various aspects of Rustin Cohle help us better understand how we can justifiably think of ourselves as being one continuous person despite our having undergone various changes.

A Story of Three Rusts

Rustin Cohle, or Rust, is identifiable as being one character by looking at the script of *True Detective* and seeing the lines of text that only Rust will say. Although not a necessary condition for the existence of a single Rust, the fact that Rust is played by only one actor, Matthew McConaughey, further buttresses the initial intuition that there is only one Rust. Yet, Rust is arguably not the same character throughout the first season. The radical variations between the different characteristics Rust exhibits allow us to think that there is more than one Rust. In fact, we can identify at least three distinct non-identical Rusts, whom we'll label *Taxman*, *Belligerent*, and *Patient*.

Taxman

There are some physical traits indicative of Taxman: his bird tattoo on his right arm, a clean-shaven appearance, and a large writing ledger usually within reach at a crime scene. These physical traits are not what stir our fascination with Taxman as a character, however. Instead, we are drawn in by his mental attributes, which we come to learn about through his incisive comments.

What also draws us to Taxman is his potentially nihilistic attitude. In the first episode, "The Long Bright Dark," he expresses this through his disavowal of human society when he states, "It's all one ghetto, man … a giant gutter in outer space." It would be a mistake, however, to think that Taxman endorses *active* nihilism of the sort that incites destructive behavior. If Taxman advocated for the world's destruction, then this perspective would be at odds with his active attempt to prevent harm to women and children in the Yellow King case. But he is highly involved in the investigation, to the extent of suffering various injuries himself. Although his self-destructive inclinations might be consistent with active nihilism, his willingness to protect others indicates that he is not content to watch everything be destroyed.

We gain additional insight into how we might think of Taxman as a nihilist when he makes disparaging remarks about religious practitioners. In particular, among his many disdainful comments are his observations in "The Locked Room" about how religion assists some people in obtaining a moral compass:

> If the only thing keeping a person decent is the expectation of divine reward then, brother, that person is a piece of shit. And I'd like to get as many of them in the open as possible. … You gotta get together, tell yourself stories that violate every law of the universe just to get through the goddamn day? What's that say about your reality?

The form of nihilism that is consistent with these observations is *reactionary* rather than active. Instead of thinking we ought to engage in destructive acts, Taxman reacts to the apparent ugliness and meaninglessness of the world.

This reactionary interpretation is consistent with his acknowledgment that human society is a gutter filled with waste, bad men who harm others. But Taxman does not think that we should sit passively waiting for bad men to enter our homes. Rather, he states that "The world needs bad men. We keep the other bad men from the door" ("The Locked Room").

Put mildly, these observations—of human society being a gutter, people requiring superstition to be moral, and recognizing our own badness—support a general view that humans are probably not the best things to come into existence. We see this view further expressed in Taxman's recommendation in "Haunted Houses" to the woman identified as having Munchausen by proxy syndrome, "The newspapers are gonna be tough on you. And prison is very,

very hard on people who hurt kids. If you get the opportunity, you should kill yourself."

Although Taxman's observations and his sanctimonious recommendation have much in common with nihilism, Taxman's view is more consistent with *anti-natalism*, which maintains that bringing a human into existence just creates additional suffering in the world. Instead of thinking that we should get rid of those humans who are already living, as the nihilist might have it, the anti-natalist maintains that we should strive to be compassionate and caring toward those who currently exist while not bringing any additional humans into existence. In doing so, we should await our own extinction. This is the view held by Taxman when he claims in "The Long Bright Dark":

> I think human consciousness is a tragic misstep in evolution. We became too self-aware. Nature created an aspect of nature separate from itself; we are creatures that should not exist by natural law. We are things that labor under the illusion of having a self. This accretion of sensory experience and feelings, programmed with total assurance that we are each somebody, when in fact everybody is nobody. I think the honorable thing for our species to do is to deny our programming, stop reproducing. Walk hand in hand into extinction.

To summarize, Taxman is someone who believes that human society is a waste, that religion reveals a person's weaknesses, that we are inherently flawed, and that things would be better if we didn't exist. Although we are drawn to him, even Taxman acknowledges in "The Long Bright Dark" that he's "bad at parties." Taxman, however, is not the only Rust. There are two more. Let's see whether they'd be good party guests.

Belligerent

In addition to Taxman's clean-cut appearance and anti-natalist leanings, we see another Rust: shaggy, long-haired, dirty, and drunk. Let's call this Rust *Belligerent*. Instead of being directly involved in the Yellow King case, Belligerent is interviewed by Detectives Gilbough and Papania as possibly being the Yellow King himself. This accusation is a result of Belligerent's deceiving

Gilbough and Papania into believing that he has been out of Louisiana tending to his ill father. While attempting to deceive Gilbough and Papania, without incriminating himself, Belligerent begins waxing metaphysical in "The Secret Fate of All Life":

> In eternity, where there is no time, nothing can grow. Nothing can become. Nothing changes. So death created time to grow the things that it would kill ... and you are reborn but into the same life that you've always been born into. ... You're trapped ... like a nightmare you keep waking up into.

Although Belligerent appears to share much of the same despairing attitude about existence that Taxman expresses, Belligerent's claims are mostly directed toward himself, rather than at society and humanity in general, as expressed in "The Locked Room":

> To realize that all your life ... it was all the same thing. It was all the same dream, a dream that you had inside a locked room, a dream about being a person. And like a lot of dreams there's a monster at the end of it.

It is here in his depression that he hides behind Lone Star beer and American Spirit cigarettes, appearing to no longer want to know any deep truth about the world or reality or himself. As he explains in "The Secret Fate of All Life":

> Fuck, I don't want to know anything anymore. This is a world where nothing is solved. Someone once told me that time is a flat circle. Everything we've ever done or will do, we're gonna do over and over and over again. And that little boy and that little girl, they're gonna be in that room again and again and again forever.

These metaphysical musings are consistent with the crises that one has in realizing that to confront the existential abyss is to converse with Friedrich Nietzsche's (1844–1900) demon, who constrains you to eternally reexperience your horrors and says:

> This life as you now live it and have lived it, you will have to live once more and innumerable times more; and there will be nothing new in it, but every pain and every joy and every thought and sigh and everything unutterably small or great in your life will have to return to you, all in the same succession and sequence—even this spider and this moonlight between the trees, and even this moment

and I myself. The eternal hourglass of existence is turned upside down again and again, and you with it, speck of dust![1]

Such an experience could certainly lead one to a state of mental and emotional paralysis of the kind we observe during Belligerent's interview. If Belligerent is right in thinking that anyone's efforts to save those doomed children are futile, then we would expect Belligerent to abandon the Yellow King case altogether. Yet, Belligerent actively deceives the interviewers into believing that he has been out of Louisiana tending to his ill father, when, in fact, he has been developing his theory about the whereabouts of the Yellow King and the missing children.

This deception provides insight into who Belligerent is. Rather than thinking of Belligerent as a deceitful drunk, he is perhaps better characterized as a vigilante, willing to go against his previous training and commitment to the police force. It is in this vigilante attempt to preserve future generations that Belligerent differs from Taxman. Whereas Taxman appears to welcome the demise of humankind while at the same time adhering to the general ideology of the police task force, Belligerent schemes to ensure that the future is secure without working within the confines of his professional obligations.

Both Taxman and Belligerent are defined in terms of their relationship to the Yellow King case, but there is more to a person than professional activities. There is also a set of character traits that shape the values that result in Taxman's and Belligerent's willingness to pursue the Yellow King case in different ways. In Taxman's case, it's his anti-natalism and concern for professional duty that lead him to adhere to professional protocol, while Belligerent's vigilantism leads him to overthrow professional mores. But what happens once the case is over? What remains of them when there is no longer a case? What remains is quite different from either Taxman or Belligerent. We get an insight into what, or better yet *who*, remains in our consideration of the third identifiable Rust.

Patient

Take away the raped and tortured victims, the occult imagery, and the catacombs of Carcosa, and what is left of Rust? Toward the end of the first season of *True Detective*, in "Form and Void," we meet a Rust who awakens from a coma after having been stabbed by Errol Childress. Let's call this Rust *Patient*. From his hospital bed, Patient reports on his experience of the coma:

> There was a moment, I know, when I was under in the dark, that something ... whatever I'd been reduced to, not even consciousness, a vague awareness in the dark, and I could feel my definitions fading ... I could feel, man, and I knew, I knew my daughter waited for me there. So clear. I could feel her. ... It was like I was a part of everything that I ever loved, and we were. ... And all I had to do was let go and I did. I said, "Darkness, yeah, yeah." And I disappeared. But I could still feel her love there, even more than before. Nothing. There was nothing but that love. Then I woke up.

These ruminations of slipping into darkness and seeing love are similar to reports given by mystics who report losing themselves to experience the love of God, the Universe, or All—whatever their mystical framework happens to be. For example, the Persian mystic Mansur al-Hallaj (858–922) poetically explained his own mystical experience:

> Love is that you remain standing
> In front of your Beloved.
> When you are deprived of all your attributes,
> Then His attributes become your qualities.
> Between me and You, there is only me.
> Take away the me, so only you remain.
> I am the Supreme Reality.[2]

Although al-Hallaj writes about the mystical connection he experiences with God, we see something similar in Patient's experience. Instead of coming to see God once he dissolves into the darkness, Patient comes to experience only the love of his daughter. It is here in the darkness that he comes to see that the only thing that exists is that love. By experiencing only that love, he comes to see that he *is* that love. It is in this mystical experience that he not only awakens to the deep truth of who he is but is also filled with hope that awakens him from the coma. The hope he feels after having experienced the deep truth of who he is remains with him once he convinces Marty to take him from the hospital. No longer anti-natalist, no longer vigilante, but now a mystic who has awakened to the oldest story of light versus dark. It is from this mystical stance that Rust claims in the season finale, "Once there was only dark. If you ask me, the light is winning."

Three in One

We should not be surprised that the first season of *True Detective* ends on a mystical note. From the very first episode, the show is infused with mystical and occult tones. For instance, when we are shown the body of Dora Lange, who has been ritualistically murdered, her head has been crowned with antlers and thorns, her hands have been bound, and her body has been surrounded by devil nets. In the last episode, Rust's character makes connections to occult lore that incorporate three-faced or three-headed gods (the Slavic three-headed god Triglav, for example). Whereas each Rust is distinct, they are all properly thought of as Rust because they share many of the same characteristics, experiences, and memories. For example, all three are originally from Texas, transferred from Louisiana, have divorced parents, and were traumatized by the accidental death of the same daughter, Sophia. They also share in the experiences of having killed a meth dealer who injected his own daughter with drugs and having spent time in a mental hospital in Lubbock. So, like mythological three-faced figures, Rust has three distinct features while at the same time it is appropriate to think of him as a single individual.

We shouldn't, however, think of Rust in mystical terms. Because Rust is similar enough to each of us in his development of these distinct personae, we shouldn't explain these disparities in a way that is not applicable to us. We do not seek mystical explanations to understand how we undergo changes, and so we should not seek a mystical explanation to understand Rust.

The Puzzle of Personal Identity

The beginning of this chapter posed multiple questions that provide insight into our understanding of what it means to be a person. The most prominent is the "reidentificaiton question": What are the conditions under which a person at one point in time is properly reidentified at another point in time?[3] When applied to the case of Rust, the question becomes: What are the conditions under which Rust at one point in time is properly reidentified at another point in time? In particular, how might we identify Taxman, Belligerent, and Patient each as properly Rust despite them existing at different times and having different characteristics?

Brute Physicalist Account

One attempt to answer this question is the brute physicalist account—the self goes with the body. There are two key components of the view. First, according to Bernard Williams (1929–2003), the physical body is necessary for there to be a self.[4] What happens to the physical body can be taken to be what happens to the self. Second, according to A. J. Ayer (1910–1989), our identity through time is dependent upon the identity of our bodies.[5] We can then apply these two points to our understanding of Rust. When Rust's body received the bird tattoo on his right arm, it was Rust who received the bird tattoo. Rust continues to be Rust so long as he has the same body, which can be identified as the body with the bird tattoo on the right arm. We might be inclined to think that Taxman, Belligerent, and Patient are the same person since each one bears the same bird tattoo.

Although this view is intuitive, it does not accommodate all our intuitions about the self. In particular, the brute physicalist view fails to accommodate the intuition that someone with the same body can change. So, although we might want to say that Taxman, Belligerent, and Patient are the same person because they have the same body in the relevant sense, the brute physicalist account does not account for how they each have different mental attitudes. For example, Taxman has the desire to successfully close the Yellow King case while working within the protocol of the police department and lacks the desire to drink alcohol. Belligerent exhibits the same desire to successfully close the Yellow King case but is not concerned about whether or not he is doing so within the purview of the police department, and he certainly desires alcohol. Both Taxman and Belligerent exhibit the same bird tattoo and, therefore, are taken to have the same body, but they have different desires and preferences. Contemporary philosopher L. A. Paul would say these different desires and results are likely the result of them having undergone *transformative experiences*—those experiences that shape one's desires and preferences, which can alter future decisions.[6] These sorts of experiences, however, do not require any physical alteration to the body. It would appear, then, that the brute physicalist account is not sufficient for understanding how there are three different Rusts while each possesses many of the same physical characteristics as the others.

Psychological Continuity Account

If it's not the body that determines who we are, perhaps it's our psychological states. This is a view that goes back to John Locke (1632–1704): "*personal identity* consists not in the Identity of [Body], but ... in the Identity of Consciousness."[7] In other words, it's the relationship between mental properties (such as memories) and personality traits that determines how we should go about identifying you as the same you at two different times.

In the case of Rust, all three Rusts have the same memory of Sophia dying in a car accident and, despite their many differences, they also share the common personality traits of quick-wittedness, focus, and diligence. The changes in Rust's mental characteristics over time would accommodate our intuition that people change despite having the same bodies, which allows us to understand how Taxman, Belligerent, and Patient are different individuals. At which point, though, do they become different people? Since they share many of the same experiences, characteristics, and memories, it is unclear how we are to differentiate them. Furthermore, since they are mental instantiations and not physical bodies, it is possible to have all three Rusts existing in the same body and, oddly, at the same time. By appealing to the psychological account, there is no restriction on how many Rusts there can be in a single body at any moment. This, too, is an odd way of thinking about the self. For this reason, the psychological continuity account does not adequately accommodate our intuitions about what a person is and how persons change.

Narrative Account

A third possible solution, the narrative account, states that we should think of our selves as narrators of a general storyline that we can think of as our lives. This allows us to create and recreate ourselves anew throughout our lives. It is important to consider this third alternative since both the brute physicalist and the psychological continuity account result in unintuitive descriptions of the self. The brute physicalist account does not accommodate the intuition that we can undergo changes even when our bodies remain the same. The psychological continuity account allows for the possibility of multiple selves occupying the same body at the same time. The narrative account overcomes these difficulties.

First, the narrative account can explain how we undergo changes even when our bodies remain the same. For example, Taxman chooses to quit the police department the day he and Hart have their fist fight. After leaving the department, he goes on to become a bartender, and, in effect, chooses to become the individual we've labeled Belligerent. Both Taxman and Belligerent have the same identifiable body, but they are very different people. The narrative account can explain how Rust made a decision to change his main occupation, give into his desires to drink, and become even more of a recluse.

Second, the narrative account does not result in the possibility of multiple selves occupying the same body at the same time, since it does not state that we are only our psychological characteristics. By thinking of our selves as the sole narrator of our lives, we can then understand Rust as the narrator of his life, which results in him becoming Taxman after having the traumatic experience of his daughter dying and spending time in a mental institute. Through the choices he makes while a detective in Louisiana, Rust then becomes Belligerent. Similarly, Rust then makes the choice to further pursue the Yellow King case in a way that results in him landing in the hospital as Patient, which results in his mystical revelations. But all of these are the same narrator, Rust, because this is the same story lived and told, in which each instance of Rust is a different phase or, to continue the literary metaphor, chapter of his life. Each chapter, however, occurs at a different time. For this reason, the same challenges facing the psychological continuity account do not befall the narrative account.

Where to Now?

Rust, in many ways, is like us. He has gone through significant experiences that shape his various preferences, desires, and characteristics. Each component modifies the very choices Rust has made in his life in a way similar to how our experiences modify the sorts of choices we are willing to make. The choices we make, however, shape who we become. We should not forget, though, that we make our own choices. Like Rust, we have the capacity to make choices that will make us very different people from who we might otherwise have become. In other words, we are the narrators of our own futures, with the ability to shape who we want to become. The difference between Rust and us, however, is that Rust's story is over. What will be your next chapter? To answer the very first question of this chapter, you need to answer: Who do you wish to become?

Notes

1. Friedrich Nietzsche, *The Gay Science*, trans. Walter Kaufmann (New York: Vintage Books, 1974), aphorism 341.
2. Andrew Harvey, *The Essential Mystics: The Soul's Journey into Truth* (London: Castle Books, 1998), 144.
3. Marya Schectman, *The Constitution of Selves* (Ithaca: Cornell University Press, 1996), 7.
4. Bernard Williams, *Problems of the Self* (Cambridge: Cambridge University Press, 1973).
5. A. J. Ayer, *Language, Truth, and Logic* (London: Gollancz, 1936).
6. L. A. Paul, *Transformative Experience* (Oxford: Oxford University Press, 2015).
7. John Locke, *Essay Concerning Human Understanding* (Oxford: Oxford University Press,1979), 342.

12

"The Light Is Winning"

Sarah K. Donovan

It's an understatement to say that Rustin Cohle is intense.[1] The "taxman" sets himself apart from the norm and doesn't shy away from speaking hard truths. Only Cohle would shut down his friend Hart's emotional outpouring to him about his failing marriage with "it's none of my business" ("Who Goes There"). But Cohle speaks out often and loudly not because he is a gadfly or a narcissist but because, unlike Hart, he is trying to be authentic. In season one of *True Detective*, we watch him evolve from a man who is slowly suffocating under the weight of the world to one who can shoulder it. His metamorphosis is existential. By the end of the season, when he proclaims that the "light is winning" ("Form and Void"), Cohle has arrived.

Stories to Keep Children Busy

Cohle is in the throes of an existential crisis. Existentialism is a school of philosophy that is best summed up by the oft-repeated phrase "existence precedes essence." Some of the more well-known philosophers and literary authors associated with existentialism, such as Friedrich Nietzsche (1844–1900), Jean-Paul Sartre (1905–1980), and Simone de Beauvoir (1908–1986), reject the idea that anything metaphysical—such as God—created humans to be one

True Detective and Philosophy: A Deeper Kind of Darkness, First Edition.
Edited by Jacob Graham and Tom Sparrow.
© 2018 John Wiley & Sons Ltd. Published 2018 by John Wiley & Sons Ltd.

way or another. You exist, and only then do you define—for yourself—who you are. In fact, for these philosophers, God does not exist at all because nothing like God, or a soul, or an overarching meaning or essence, exists either here on earth or in an afterlife (which is not real). Cohle rejects the existence of God often and loudly with dismissive comments that cast religious people as having a propensity for "fairy tales," as he says in "Seeing Things." Cohle thinks that God is a lie and a story we tell ourselves to feel safe. While visiting a revival tent with Hart, Cohle says of the preacher's sermon, and the people gathered, "What's it say about life, hmm? You gotta get together, tell yourself stories that violate every law of the universe just to get through the goddamn day?" Of the relationship between the churchgoers and the preacher, Cohle gives a secular, psychological interpretation: "Transference of fear and self-loathing to an authoritarian vessel. It's catharsis. He absorbs their dread with his narrative." Nietzsche, Sartre, and Beauvoir would agree.

Cohle also reveals his views about religion in what he doesn't say. In "The Long Bright Dark," when Cohle and Hart follow up on a lead on the missing Fontenot girl, they ask a local preacher about the handmade wooden structures they keep finding. The preacher says that he learned about them from his Old Aunty, whose devotion to Christianity was mixed with Santería. Old Aunty called the structures "devil nets" and said they stop the devil from getting you while you sleep. The preacher recalls with affection that, when he was a kid, Old Aunty would tell him these stories as he tied the devil-nets, and he thought that both the stories and the nets were just something for children to do to keep them busy. As he says this, we follow Cohle's gaze to a cross that is, like the devil nets, bound into its shape with a tie. The parallel is clear.

The Family Man

Both Nietzsche and Sartre describe the dread and anxiety that result from rejecting the existence of God. For many existentialists, to reject metaphysics is also to deny that we are born with a core self, an essence, or a predesigned purpose. The knowledge that we create our own meaning is, initially, an enormous burden. Sartre believes that it will be paralyzing before it can be recast as liberating, and Nietzsche describes it as deadening and dulling to us before it can make us creative and alive.

Most existentialists agree it is harsh to realize that we must create meaning out of nothing, with no God to approve of our actions and nowhere to go when we die. Most of us choose to ignore this fact, or retreat into a position of inauthenticity or denial of our existential freedom. Hart, in his insistence that he is a "family man," is an example of someone in denial.

Sartre's ontology, or his study of being, in his magnum opus *Being and Nothingness*,[2] helps us to understand what Hart is trying to escape through his strong identification as a family man. Sartre's philosophical study of being (as opposed to a scientific study in a lab) describes existence, at its most basic and abstract level, as broadly divided into being-in-itself and being-for-itself. There are unconscious things (being-in-itself) and there is human consciousness (being-for-itself). Humans are, of course, being-in-itself (we have bodies, after all) and being-for-itself, but the two ways of being are distinct.

In fact, being-for-itself actually has no being at all. Sartre characterizes human consciousness as an activity, or a no-thing-ness, through which we seek meaning. It is here that Sartre locates human freedom, and he describes why we run away from it and embrace inauthenticity. We can think of consciousness as transcendence. This means that if we really are, as human consciousness, an activity, we are constantly outside ourselves, seeking meaning in the world. Consciousness really is no-where in particular (because it is "out there," constantly seeking), and it is certainly no-thing (because it is an activity, not a thing). We cling to identity and grand narratives about meaning because we seek comfort in the face of no-thing-ness.

Hart is inauthentic in identifying himself as a "family man" because there has never been a person who is a "family man" in any strong sense. No one has a core, an essence, or a stable identity (the only stability is that consciousness is a constantly shifting activity). To say Hart is a family man is a misunderstanding of human consciousness, which, as an activity, cannot be any one identity. "Family man" is just one social role, among many, that a person might play at any given moment. For Sartre, it is as fleeting and impermanent as the shifting activity of consciousness.

Hart's moments of infidelity are opportunities for him to reject his set identity, recognize his freedom, and take responsibility for it. Yet he chooses to cling to his identity and embrace inauthenticity. In "Seeing Things," an older, divorced Hart goes on and on about the importance of family and his role as a family man. In his interview with detectives Gilbough and Papania, Hart says, "You gotta decompress before you can go being a family man." This is punctuated by a flashback to a younger, married Hart, engaging in behavior not typically associated with a traditional view of a family man. He is driving drunk and stopping to call his younger mistress in the hopes of sex involving bondage (which we are led to assume he doesn't do with his wife, as a family man). Going back to the older Hart, he says, "It's for your wife and kids too. You gotta take your release where you find it. ... In the end it's for the good of the family." In instances like these, Hart is determined to believe a narrative that isn't even consistent. Sartre would say that Hart is not alone in preferring deception to responsibility for freedom.

A younger Cohle tries to point out Hart's inauthenticity when they are grabbing a quick lunch at a roadside café in "The Locked Room." Hart accuses Cohle of being obsessive about work and claims that he is not, himself, obsessive. Hart says, "I keep things even, separate." He asks Cohle, "You know the real difference between you and me?" to which Cohle responds, "Yup, denial." As usual, Cohle pushes Hart to see that his identification as "family man" and "God-fearing" are inauthentic and a denial of his freedom.

His ex-wife, Maggie, also captures Hart's inauthenticity in her interview with Gilbough and Papania when she says of Hart, "Marty's single biggest problem ... he never really knew himself. So he never knew what to want" ("Haunted Houses"). But Hart is not a lost cause. While the older Hart still has moments in which he holds on to the illusion of himself as a family man, he also has insights where he acknowledges his shortcomings. As he says of his family in 2012, "My true failure was inattention" ("Who Goes There"). Though far from existential authenticity, the older Hart is at least grappling with the reality of his life as opposed to his inauthentic storyline of "family man."

The Poison of Nihilism

Cohle agrees with the existentialists that God does not exist, and he tries to be authentic, but he embraces his dread rather than his freedom. This leads him to say things like, "I think human consciousness is a tragic misstep in evolution. ... We are things that labor under the illusion of having a self. ... The honorable thing for our species to do is to deny our programming, stop reproducing" ("The Long Bright Dark"). Cohle is paralyzed, pessimistic, and misanthropic.

Cohle can pinpoint the moment his despair became acute: when his two-year-old daughter, Sophia, died in a tragic accident, hit by a car as she pedaled her tricycle out of the family's driveway. She was vulnerable, and Cohle feels like he failed to protect her. She is, understandably, a big piece of his ongoing crisis and lack of faith that life has any meaning.

Cohle has woven a narrative for himself around her death that confirms his pessimism and despair. In "Seeing Things," an older Cohle says:

> You know how I think about my daughter now ... she was spared. Sometimes I feel grateful. Doctor said she didn't feel a thing. Went straight into a coma, and then, somewhere in that blackness she slipped off into another, deeper kind. Isn't that a beautiful way to go out? Painlessly, as a happy child.

Continuing this line of thought, Cohle says that adults have a harder time letting go—especially in the face of how meaningless it all is. "As for my daughter," he says, "she, uh, she spared me the sin of being a father." Cohle's words echo the wisdom of Silenus, an ancient mythical creature whom Nietzsche references in *The Birth of Tragedy*.[3] Silenus says that it would be best for all humans not to be born, and the second best possibility is to die soon. Cohle's despair makes him feel this must be true.

In *Thus Spoke Zarathustra*, Nietzsche provides us with an image that captures the thread of Cohle's suffocating narrative. Nietzsche describes a tightrope walker who must go from point A to point B on a tightrope. Along the way, he is challenged on the rope by a fellow walker (called "the spirit of gravity") who taunts him with poisonous comments, fills him with doubt, and ultimately jumps over him in order to block him from reaching the other side. It is an image about the hard road we travel from the rejection of a God, or an overarching meaning of life (point A), through the overwhelming dread that ensues (represented by the person on the tightrope who hopes to block you or even make you fall to your death), to the intentional creation of meaning in the face of such nothingness (point B). Cohle is balanced on the tightrope, listening to the spirit of gravity, and he is sick with poison.[4]

Cohle even speaks like Nietzsche's spirit of gravity and Silenus himself when, in "The Long Bright Dark," he says humans should "walk hand in hand into extinction, one last midnight—brothers and sisters opting out of a raw deal." When Hart asks, in response, why he continues to live, Cohle does not pretend it is out of hope that life has meaning. He just says that he "lack[s] the constitution" for suicide.

An older Cohle holds onto this narrative about himself. During his questioning by Gilbough and Papania in "Seeing Things," Cohle describes his solitary existence and says that when you "reach a certain age, you know who you are. I know who I am, and after all these years there's a victory in that."

When Hart and Cohle reconnect in "After You've Gone," Cohle convinces Hart that the killings have continued by showing him the stolen video documenting Marie Fontenot's brutal rape and murder. When Hart asks Cohle why he came back, Cohle says, "My life has been a circle of violence and degradation, as long as I can remember. I'm ready to tie it off." Cohle has had enough of his life; he is trapped in his despair and choking on its poison.

The Vulnerable Hold the Antidote

Cohle's actions throughout the series belie his proclamations about the futility of existence, however. His obsession with the Dora Lange case is not just about trying to catch a killer. Cohle is trying to understand an uglier, darker, and crueler kind of killing— that of vulnerable women and children. When he and Hart first investigated the Dora Lange case, it was Cohle who pushed them to uncover evidence of other missing women. Cohle pushes them to look into Marie Fontenot's disappearance, and into the death of Reanne Olivier. It is Cohle's persistence that led to the dramatic rescue of the kidnapped children in "The Secret Fate of All Life." In spite of his professions about life's futility, Cohle cares about these women and children, and he feels a responsibility for them.

In her magnum opus, *The Second Sex*, Simone de Beauvoir[5] applies existential theory to describe the perceived inferiority of women throughout history. Her feminist, existential perspective clarifies Cohle's focus on women and children. Beauvoir believes that men are taught to be active subjects while women are taught to be passive. As active subjects, men are more likely to engage in a self-defined, existential project. As passive subjects, women are more likely to be defined by others and objectified. But there is no essence to maleness or femaleness, so women can be just as active as men, if they take charge of their existential project.

As Cohle investigates the disappearances and murders, he focuses on the helplessness and objectification of the victims. Cohle, like Beauvoir, recognizes that not all people can pursue their projects equally. He understands that people who lack social power and wealth are more vulnerable to other people's projects. We can understand his concern with women and children as a part of his own existential crisis. As Sartre and Beauvoir believed, when the existential freedom of others is threatened, our own freedom is threatened as well.

It is not just the young Cohle who cares about the vulnerable. Cohle remains consistently obsessed. In 2002, years after Cohle and Hart locate Reggie Ledoux and "solve" the case, Cohle learns that the case is bigger than Ledoux. He starts investigating again in spite of direct orders from his superiors to desist. When Major Salter demands an explanation for Cohle's obstinate behavior, Cohle says, "Women, children disappearing. Nobody hears about … Nobody puts it together … Women and children … neither get no press. The way things in the bayou get no press" ("Haunted Houses"). Cohle wouldn't bother to continue the investigation if he really believed we are just "biological puppets" with no hope of real meaning in our lives, as he says in "The Locked Room."

We cannot underestimate the importance of his daughter to explain why Cohle cares so much. Cohle and Hart begin investigation of the Dora Lange case on Sophia's birthday, and Sophia's vulnerability seems to haunt Cohle as he investigates. We see how important Sophia is to his actions when he shows up drunk at Hart's house for dinner with Hart's family—Cohle thought he couldn't face a happy family sober.

Cohle gives us a further glimpse into the early depths of his despair after Sophia's death when he talks, in "Seeing Things," about how he spiraled out of control, lost his marriage, became addicted to drugs, and ended up killing a man. Yet, even as he took another human's life, Cohle was acting out of concern for the vulnerable. He tells us, "I emptied a nine into a crankhead for injecting his infant daughter with crystal." Even in a drug-induced craze, Cohle's impulse was to protect those who cannot protect themselves.

Hart, in spite of his spotty self-reflection, has moments of insight about Cohle. It is Hart who recognizes that Cohle's actions indicate that he has not really given up hope that life has meaning. In "The Locked Room," after months of listening to Cohle's pronouncements about the absurdity of existence and its lack of meaning, Hart says to him: "For a guy who sees no point in existence, you sure fret about it an awful lot." Cohle resists succumbing to despair because of the vulnerable people to whom he "owes a debt" ("After You've Gone").

The Head of the Snake

Enter Nietzsche's eternal return as a framework for Cohle's struggles. For Nietzsche, you cannot truly love life unless you can see it for what it really is and still love it. In fact, you have to love life so much that you will it eternally, in all of its sheer beauty and utter horror. Nietzsche uses the imagery of peaks, valleys, and abysses to describe the spectrum of life, which contains both intense joy and unbearable suffering. For Nietzsche, you have to confront the low points, or abysses, in life but not let them consume you. In fact, you have to will both joy and suffering eternally. Of course, this does not mean that you condone atrocities but that you find a way to live and love life alongside a real knowledge of the utter savagery that happens (intentional or natural). Nietzsche calls it his most difficult thought, and Cohle is in its throes.

The meth cook Reggie Ledoux is a mouthpiece for a warped version of the eternal return, and at least one embodiment of "the spirit of gravity" that weighs Cohle down. Before Hart kills him, Ledoux says to Cohle that he saw him in a dream. In "The Secret Fate of All Life," he says, "You're in Carcosa now, with me. He sees you ... You'll do this again. Time is a flat circle." Cohle replies, disparagingly, "Is that Nietzsche? Shut the fuck up!" Ledoux is speaking like Nietzsche's spirit of gravity when it describes its defeatist version of the eternal return.[6]

Indeed, this warped version of the eternal return infects Cohle. He speaks in terms similar to Ledoux when he recalls the dramatic rescue of the children to Gilbough and Papania. He says to the detectives, "Someone once told me that time is a flat circle. Everything we've ever done or will do, we're gonna do over and over and over again. And that little boy and girl, they're gonna be in that room again and again and again forever" ("The Secret Fate of All Life"). The "spirit of gravity" is a name for what holds the existentialist in a state of defeat and anxiety in the absence of God: it is the enemy on the tightrope. It is the dread and anxiety we feel at the horrors of life, of which Cohle has seen more than most could bear.

Reggie Ledoux, and all the evil he caused, is an apt embodiment of this spirit. When Cohle, in "The Locked Room," describes how he imagines that a person on the brink of death welcomes death, he says that they understand in that moment that life is a dream, "a dream about being a person," but that, "like a lot of dreams there's a monster at the end of it." As Cohle says this, we are shown an image of Ledoux, dirty, in his underpants, wearing a gas mask, and carrying a machete. Ledoux is a picture of the alienation and raw violence that would drag anyone into doubt about human nature, but Cohle has more monsters to meet before he confronts his own dread.

Nietzsche gives us an image of the eternal return in *Thus Spoke Zarathustra* that fits Cohle's existential struggle. In "On the Vision and the Riddle," Zarathustra describes a shepherd who, while asleep, had a snake crawl into his throat, bite him, and hold him tight. The shepherd can either choke on the snake or bite its head off. Zarathustra describes the choking man's face as filled with utter horror—he is suffocating and gagging. Zarathustra tries to help but realizes that only the shepherd can help himself. Zarathustra tells him to bite the head off the snake. The shepherd does it and stands up, as Zarathustra describes, transformed and laughing.[7]

The snake represents the necessity of affirming all aspects of life and willing them eternally. Who would not be sickened and choked by the thought of affirming all the suffering in life along with all the joy? When the shepherd bites the snake, he has become strong enough for that kind of affirmation. He doesn't condone suffering, but he can shoulder it because of his profound love for life itself. Throughout the first season of *True Detective*, Cohle is the shepherd who is choking on all that is bitter and ugly in the world. He is struggling to find the strength to kill the snake.

"The Light Is Winning"

This leads us to Errol Childress. He is the hyperbolic monster at the end of the dream; he is the specter of nihilism and suffering. Reggie Ledoux's monstrosity pales by comparison. Cohle has been staring into the abyss of human suffering for decades, but, when he goes to Carcosa, he falls deep within it. And Childress waits for him at the bottom. Their encounter ends with a violent, crippling battle and Childress' death.

But Cohle's story doesn't end there. Cohle and Hart know that Childress was not a lone wolf. They have proof that the Tuttle family is linked to the murders, but the family's power actively erases any connections that Cohle and Hart are able to draw. Like any truly frightening monster, this one cannot be killed—Childress was just one of its many heads. The circle of violence and destruction is not broken by Childress' death. As Cohle says to Hart from his hospital bed in "Form and Void," "We didn't get 'em all." In the face of this, we expect Cohle's despair to deepen, but it doesn't. In fact, Cohle discovered more than just a monster at the bottom of the abyss.

In the final scene of the season, Cohle and Hart have a cryptic conversation that is couched in terms of the battle between light and dark. Cohle is still reeling from his near-death experience, in which he was immersed in "the dark," and could feel the presence and love of his deceased daughter and father. He says that "I was a part of everything that I ever loved, and we were all, the three of us, just, just fadin' out. And all I had to do was let go and I did. ... And I disappeared. But I could still feel her love there, even more than before. Nothing. There was nothing but that love. Then I woke up." While he had earlier proclaimed that death confirms the futility of existence, he discovers now that he was wrong. Cohle traveled deep within the abyss of human misery and suffering and he found, at the end, not only a monster but pure love as well. In fact, it was the monster that led him to the feeling of love. In that moment, he finally "lets go" and "bites the head off the snake." The circle is complete as he has found Sophia, his joy and love, in the suffering of the abyss.

While Cohle finds his meaning and begins a new narrative, it is not based in God or the afterlife. Rather, it is grounded in the memory of the genuine love that he once felt with his daughter. He now understands that there is real love amid suffering and that even in the darkest night there are stars. The final lines of dialogue crystallize his new, existential optimism. Looking at the stars in the dark sky, Hart says, "Well, I know we ain't in Alaska, but it appears to me that the dark has a lot more territory." Cohle thinks about this and says, "You lookin' at it wrong—the sky, I mean. Once there was only dark. If you ask me, the light is winning." In this moment, Cohle jumps over the spirit of gravity and finds solid ground on the other side of the tightrope.

Notes

1. A shorter, earlier version of this book chapter was published on the ANDPHILOSOPHY.COM site of the Blackwell Philosophy and Pop Culture series: https://andphilosophy.com/2014/06/11/true-detective-and-philosophy-the-light-is-winning.
2. If you are just beginning to read Sartre, you might start with the introduction by Thomas Flynn in the online *Stanford Encyclopedia of Philosophy* (http://plato.stanford.edu/entries/sartre). You will also find

there an entry on Friedrich Nietzsche by Robert Wicks (http://plato. stanford.edu/entries/nietzsche) and an entry on "Nietzsche's Life and Work" by R. Lanier Anderson (https://plato.stanford.edu/entries/ nietzsche-life-works).

3. Friedrich Nietzsche, *The Birth of Tragedy, or: Hellenism and Pessimism*, in *The Basic Writings of Nietzsche*, trans. and ed. Walter Kaufmann (New York: Modern Library, 1992), 42.

4. Friedrich Nietzsche, *Thus Spoke Zarathustra: A Book for None and All*, trans. and ed. Walter Kaufmann (New York: Penguin, 1978), 19–20.

5. For a clear introduction to Beauvoir's work, see Debra Bergoffen's article on Simone de Beauvoir in the *Stanford Encyclopedia of Philosophy* (http://plato.stanford.edu/entries/beauvoir).

6. Zarathustra debates the nature of time and eternal return with the spirit of gravity in Nietzsche, *Thus Spoke Zarathustra*, 155–158.

7. Ibid., 159–160.

13

The Tragic Misstep

Consciousness, Free Will, and the Last Midnight

Daniel P. Malloy

A central concern of Rust Cohle's brand of pessimism is the nature of consciousness. It's not just that the world is generally a terrible place; it's that we're aware of it in a way that we shouldn't be. In "The Long Bright Dark," Cohle calls human self-consciousness "a tragic misstep in evolution." But in the same monologue Cohle claims that we should "deny our programming, stop reproducing. Walk hand in hand into extinction, one last midnight—brothers and sisters opting out of a raw deal."

There are two problems with Cohle's contention. First, it's unclear whether, much less how, a programmed being could deny its programming. In one breath, Cohle seems to both affirm and deny that humans have free will. Everything is programmed, but the thing that's aware of its programming may be able to rise above it.

Second and similarly, he seems to both celebrate and denounce self-consciousness. It's both the cause of and the solution to the suffering that plagues the human animal. The tragic misstep of self-consciousness is both what makes us freaks of nature that can't quite fit in and what gives us the ability to escape from nature.

This chapter considers the relationship between self-consciousness and the ability to "deny our programming," or free will. The central question is whether self-consciousness grants the

True Detective and Philosophy: A Deeper Kind of Darkness, First Edition.
Edited by Jacob Graham and Tom Sparrow.
© 2018 John Wiley & Sons Ltd. Published 2018 by John Wiley & Sons Ltd.

ability to alter or deny our programming or whether it merely gives the illusion that we have such an ability. A secondary consideration is whether our possession of this ability or illusion is fortunate or not. As we'll see, Cohle's assessment of self-consciousness and free will is broadly correct, but his evaluation of self-consciousness as a "tragic misstep" is mistaken.

The Constitution for Suicide

When asked why he bothers with anything given his dour views, Rust Cohle answers that, ultimately, "it's obviously my programming, and I lack the constitution for suicide." In other words, he keeps going, doing what he does, because he doesn't have a choice. He's alive and continues to do all the things he does because his programming won't allow him to do anything else. But this is more of an excuse than an answer. We need to delve a bit deeper to uncover the answer.

Let's say that Cohle is right: we are programmed beings that, like any computer, can only do what our programming tells us. If that's the case, then we don't have choices and, by most lights, don't have free will. There are, however, some philosophers who argue that, even if we lack choices, we still retain free will. It all depends on how we understand the will and its freedom.

Cohle's understanding of free will seems to most closely align with the doctrine of radical free will. Espoused by existentialist philosopher Jean-Paul Sartre (1905–1980), radical free will maintains that certain kinds of beings—such as humans—have absolute and total control over themselves.[1]

There are two drawbacks to radical free will. First, it implies that all of our choices are equally valid. If there aren't reasons for our actions, then there can't be good or bad reasons either. Any choice is precisely as good as any other choice. As Sartre says, "all human activities are equivalent. ... Thus it amounts to the same thing whether one gets drunk alone or is a leader of nations."[2] When Cohle has sex with Maggie in "Haunted Houses," for instance, the reason for it is also the reason against it: he makes a choice. In this sense, radical free will and Cohle's programming theory boil down to roughly the same thing: when all choices are equally valid, all choices are equally, objectively meaningless.

However, radical free will and the programming theory do have some conflicting implications. In particular, if we are programmed beings simply carrying out our programming, then we are not responsible for what we do. Everything, including our actions and their consequences, just kind of happens. On the other hand, if we have radical free will, then it follows that we are also radically responsible. If we are in total control of ourselves, then we are responsible for everything in our lives. Each choice has consequences, and in making any choice we accept those consequences, even if they are unintended or unforeseeable. Rust and his ex-wife Claire made certain choices, such as having a child, allowing her to play on a tricycle, and living where they did. Sadly, those choices led to the death of their daughter, Sophia. If Rust and his wife are radically free, then they are responsible for Sophia's death.

Cohle's programming theory depends on a conception of free will similar to Sartre's. In contrast to Sartre, though, Cohle must conclude that we don't have free will. As we'll see, though, there are other conceptions of free will that allow us to make non-arbitrary choices and retain some level of meaning and responsibility, without overburdening us with responsibility the way radical free will does.

More than a Biological Puppet

After discovering evidence of yet another act of marital infidelity by Marty in "Haunted Houses," Maggie leaves him. Marty's repeated failures as a husband make the event all but inevitable. Maggie's choice involves manipulating Marty into leaving her, rather than making the break herself. After her liaison with Cohle in the same episode, she explains, "He'll have to go, you see, because this he won't live with."

But imagine a case where Maggie has no choice in the matter. In this scenario, her break with Marty is inevitable, whether she wants it or not. For example, suppose that Marty's one-time mistress Lisa arranges it so that, the next time Maggie finds evidence of Marty's infidelity, she will leave him. Maybe hypnosis is involved; it doesn't matter. The point is, even if Maggie has a change of heart and decides to forgive Marty, she will still leave him. Now, as it turns out, Maggie has no such change of heart. She leaves Marty by choice, in spite of the fact that she really has no choice. Maggie has no alternate possibilities, and yet she makes a free choice.

This example is a version of a scenario put forward by philosopher Harry Frankfurt and is appropriately called a Frankfurt case.[3] The point is that, even in a situation where we have no possibility but to act in a particular way, it is still possible for us to choose to act in that way and thus to be responsible for our choice.

This understanding of free will squares with Cohle's programming theory. We may indeed be biological puppets, acting and reacting solely to the tugging on our strings, but we are also free beings making choices and confronting responsibility. So, for example, let's say that Cohle is right when he says that he lacks the constitution for suicide. No matter how badly he wants to, he can't kill himself. He can still choose how to deal with that fact about himself. As it is, he seems to see it as some sort of punishment or curse—hence his sunny outlook. He could instead embrace this inability and see it as an opportunity to "bear witness," as he puts it in "The Long Bright Dark."

Nature Separate from Nature

One thing that Cohle and most people who spend any time thinking about free will seem to agree on is that it is bound up in some way with consciousness. For Cohle, the whole tragedy of human existence is summed up in a single sentence: "We became too self-aware" ("The Long Bright Dark"). But it is only thanks to our self-awareness, to our "illusion of having a self," that we can opt out of the raw deal of existing. If we didn't have self-consciousness, there wouldn't be either a need or a possibility of making that kind of choice.

Proponents of both radical free will and the middle ground of freedom-with-programming also see this connection. Sartre's notion of radical free will is based on his understanding of consciousness as the source of nothingness. That is, in a world without consciousness, everything just is what it is: being-in-itself, as Sartre called it. But the second a conscious being enters the world, a being-for-itself, it also introduces nothingness: the way things might be but aren't. For example, when Marty kills Reggie in "The Secret Fate of All Life," he does so based on the idea of a world without Reggie in it. When Cohle helps him cover up the murder, he does so based on a conception of a world where they don't get caught. Consciousness produces the way things might be, could be, ought to be. This, in turn, produces choice. We have choice because we are constantly confronted with the biggest nothing of all: our consciousness of the future. We have to keep making the future, projecting ourselves into it, imagining, planning, preparing. It's the one thing, for Sartre, that we have no choice in. As he says, "to be free is to be condemned to be free."[4] Having a self, for Sartre, isn't so much an illusion as a choice: a person can either embrace the fact of their freedom and accept responsibility for their life or they can run from it. Running doesn't change or eliminate the fact of freedom, but there are all sorts of places to hide from it.

Again, things aren't quite so bleak with the freedom-with-programming option. In Frankfurt's view, the idea of will really comes down to desire (rather than action), and freedom comes in when we distinguish two classes of desires.[5] Some desires are first-order desires: these refer to certain objects in the world. We can desire a beer, a better job, a new friend, a good fuck, or to kill. Those are all first-order desires. There are also, however, second-order desires: desires about desires, and they are the key to free will. As self-aware beings, we aren't trapped by our first-order desires. We can change them, rearrange them, prioritize them, in accordance with our second-order desires. Marty, for example, doesn't have to sleep around. He wants to, sure. But he also wants to be a good husband and father. Those are both first-order desires. Now, for most people, the desire to be a good husband and father would lead to a second-order desire: the desire *not* to desire to sleep around. Marty, on the other hand, seems to see no conflict between his various affairs and his life with Maggie and his daughters. Marty is what Frankfurt calls a "wanton." He has both first- and second-order desires, but his second-order desires never manifest themselves. He doesn't act on them or give them the power to change or reprioritize his first-order desires.

Whichever version of free will we accept, it is intimately bound to consciousness. In these examples, one cannot have the one without the other. A non-conscious being has no will and therefore cannot have free will. But also, in both of these cases, as in Cohle's view of the world, there is a causal connection between consciousness and free will. Consciousness grants free will. The difference between Cohle's view and the views of Sartre and Frankfurt has to do with their estimation of consciousness. For both Sartre and Frankfurt, consciousness is a genuine fact; it is true and important that we are conscious and self-aware beings. For Cohle, on the other hand, consciousness is either a mistake or an illusion. The resulting notion of free will is, in turn, either a mistake or an illusion.

"Everybody's Nobody"

Cohle isn't alone in his assessments of consciousness and free will. Anyone who denies that we have free will has to explain the impressions we have of making decisions, whether they are carefully planned out and thoroughly deliberated or spur-of-the-moment and impulsive. If we really are simply programmed beings, mere biological puppets, why does it seem to us that we make decisions? If we have no free will, why do we worry and fret over events that are as inevitable and predictable as the sunrise?

The short answer, offered by philosophers such as Baruch Spinoza (1632–1677) and Arthur Schopenhauer (1788–1860), is ignorance. The more thorough answer is that the impression we have of making decisions is the result of a combination of ignorance and awareness. We believe that we are in control of our actions and decisions because we do not understand their true causes. We are aware that we are acting, but we don't know why. So, we tell ourselves that our awareness of our actions is actually control over them, when, in fact, we are no more in control of ourselves than surfers are of the waves they ride.

But if we aren't in control of ourselves, what is? Cohle claims that we are programmed—largely, it seems, by evolution. We are biological puppets, doing what we can, or have to, to carry out two simple imperatives: survive and pass on our genes. In Cohle's case, having tried and failed at the second, his drive to do the first has been shaken.

Schopenhauer, on the other hand, argued that we are determined entirely by will—not free will, but merely the constantly and insatiably desiring will.[6] The will can take many forms, such as the will-to-live, the will-to-more, the will-to-pleasure, and so forth; but underneath them all is the will, eternally yearning and driving us on to the next thing that might satisfy it. This is why Schopenhauer described life as a constant oscillation between pain and boredom. Life confronts us with only two choices: the pain of not fulfilling a desire—not achieving what we will—and the boredom that follows a fulfilled desire. Rest, peace, contentment: those are things we can dream of but can't possibly achieve while we continue to be driven by the will. Every action by every character in *True Detective* can be explained in these terms, if we accept that the core of reality itself is nothing but an eternal, unquenchable will. Marty's affairs with Lisa and Beth, his murder of Reggie Ledoux, and his drinking are all attempts to quiet the never-ending will. And, predictably, they all fail.

For Spinoza, however, things are a bit less bleak. First, it's not simple will that drives us, nor some grand process such as evolution that programs us. For Spinoza, our actions are like every other event in the universe: the effects of definite causes.[7] For example, when Cohle has sex with Maggie, he doesn't simply choose to. His desire leads him to, combined with the absence of any hindrances to fulfilling that desire. But the desire itself is caused as well, by Cohle's loneliness, Maggie's attractiveness, and good old-fashioned biology. Combine those with Maggie's desire to force Marty's hand, her own attraction to Cohle, and a bit of alcohol and the result is inevitable and predictable. There's nothing mystical or mysterious or grandiose about it; it's simple cause and effect, just like everything else that's ever happened or ever will.

Opting Out

Regardless of what forces compel us, however, all of these theories agree on one thing: our impression that we make decisions is the result of our awareness of our actions combined with our ignorance of their actual causes. It also seems that, at least for Schopenhauer and Spinoza, overcoming our ignorance is the key to our escape, our freedom. In other words, the only way to be free is to become more conscious. On the surface, it seems that they agree with Cohle: the only solution is to deny our programming, go against our inclinations and impulses, and welcome the end. "Stop reproducing. Walk hand in hand into extinction, one last midnight—brothers and sisters opting out of a raw deal."

The sentiment seems, at first glance, to be very much in line with Schopenhauer's conclusions. As he understood it, once we become aware of the role of will and its seeming inescapability, the goal becomes to find some way out. Because we are conscious, we have tools at our disposal that allow us to deny our programming, to overcome the will itself. We get brief glimpses of this kind of escape when we contemplate works of art or engage in genuinely self-less actions, but those are fleeting. The only way to achieve lasting peace is to deny the will itself, and particularly the will-to-live.

It may seem, as it does to Cohle, that this way of thinking has only one logical conclusion: suicide. But Schopenhauer denies that. Suicide is not a rejection of the will-to-live, but its affirmation. When a person dies by suicide, according to Schopenhauer, they do so to escape from the pain and suffering of life. Escaping from pain and suffering is a goal that every living thing strives for, and is therefore entailed by the will-to-live. Suicide, then, is not a denial of the will-to-live; it is one tool among many for pursuing the will-to-live's goals. Denying the will-to-live instead requires living a life as devoid of the things that the will-to-live wants as possible. As Schopenhauer sees it, the self-denying path of the ascetic is the only one that offers the opportunity to find lasting peace. He would approve of the Spartan nature of Cohle's existence. Cohle's lack of possessions or attachments is an example of the only way to deny the will-to-live, according to Schopenhauer. We can't achieve tranquility or peace by fulfilling a desire. The only path to peace is to deny desire itself. We can only be tranquil by ceasing to will altogether. Stripping ourselves of desires, as Cohle has largely done, grants us the only sort of freedom Schopenhauer thinks we can have: a freedom from trouble or worry.

For Spinoza, on the other hand, once we rid ourselves of the notion of free will, we open the door to making more accurate and precise observations of ourselves and our actions, and of the causes and effects that shape our lives. By doing this, we can discover the links between the effects that are our actions and their real causes. Once those links are known, freedom of a sort becomes possible. Not freedom in the sense of free will; that, according to Spinoza, is simply nonsense. No, the kind of freedom we can achieve is a freedom from certain kinds of influences and causes. It is a negative freedom. In particular, we can be free from causes external to ourselves—free to follow our own internal promptings, the impulses and desires of our own being. If, for example, Cohle had known about Maggie's vulnerability or realized the depths of his own loneliness, that knowledge could have caused him to slam the door in her face rather than let her in that night, which, in turn, may have saved his partnership with Marty.

Apart from their denial of free will, the one thing Cohle, Schopenhauer, and Spinoza all share is the belief that the only solution to the puzzle or problem of existence is increased consciousness. Only by becoming more aware of the "raw deal" can we opt out of it. Cohle's "tragic misstep" turns out to hold the key to its own solution, and the solution to the problem of existence more generally.

"The Light Is Winning"

Either consciousness grants us free will or it causes the illusion of free will. In either case, it carries the germ of an answer to the problems that burden Cohle and the rest of us. Consciousness curses us with the struggles of daily life and the tragedies of living in this bizarre, alien landscape, and blesses us with paths to escape.

If we have free will, that means we can choose to take actions that alleviate suffering, or end it all together. Those options are available to us, and known to us, because of the tragic misstep. Without this little evolutionary error, we'd be truly and irrevocably doomed.

Imagine, for a second, a world like ours, populated by beings like us but without consciousness. The question of free will wouldn't arise for these philosophical zombies. Without consciousness, no questions would arise. Billions upon billions of such beings would be born, live a while, maybe reproduce, and then die, all in blissful ignorance of their sorry state. Only there wouldn't be any bliss or ignorance in such a world because both require consciousness. Calling a philosophical zombie ignorant is like calling a table or a chair ignorant. In the strictest sense, it's true that none of these things has any knowledge. But, looked at more closely, they also lack the capacity for knowledge itself and so can't really be ignorant.

In our own world, it's the sliver of self-awareness we've achieved that makes it possible, one way or another, to achieve some relief and respite. Of course, it's that same capacity that makes us aware that there's something to want relief and respite from. Philosophical zombies couldn't choose, but they also couldn't suffer, thus freeing them from the need to choose.

Maybe a life without either consciousness or free will wouldn't be any worse than ours. Maybe Cohle's right, and consciousness is a tragic misstep. But look at it from another angle: philosophical zombies may not have things any worse than us, but it makes very little sense to say they have things any better either. They don't suffer, but they also don't enjoy.

If, on the other hand, we are programmed, biological puppets, consciousness grants us the only relief and release possible from that. By becoming aware of our programming, by increasing our consciousness of ourselves and our environment, we change the terms of the program itself. The program says strive, reproduce, die. When we become aware, as Cohle has, that any living thing brought into this world will be instilled with the same program, and that this program of striving, reproducing, and dying has no ultimate end or purpose, we've begun reprogramming ourselves.

If the light is winning, at least in our own little corner of the universe, it's because of consciousness. Even if the light isn't winning, it's here, for a while, because of consciousness. Let it shine.

Notes

1. Jean-Paul Sartre, *Being and Nothingness*, trans. Hazel E. Barnes (New York: Washington Square Press, 1993).
2. Ibid., 797.
3. Harry Frankfurt, "Alternate Possibilities and Moral Responsibility," *Journal of Philosophy* (1969) 66.

4. Sartre, *Being and Nothingness*, 129.
5. Harry Frankfurt, "Freedom of the Will and the Concept of a Person," *Journal of Philosophy* (1971) 68.
6. Arthur Schopenhauer, *The World as Will and Representation* (2 vols.), trans. E. F. J. Payne (New York: Dover, 1966).
7. Baruch Spinoza, *Ethics*, trans. G. H. R. Parkinson (New York: Oxford University Press, 2000).

Part IV

"THIS IS MY LEAST FAVORITE LIFE"
Noir, Tragedy, and Philosopher-Detectives

14

The Tragedy of *True Detective* Season Two
Living Our "Least Favorite Lives"

Alison Horbury

According to *True Detective*'s creator, Nic Pizzolatto, season two aimed at tragedy, taking inspiration from the archetypical tragedy *Oedipus Rex* to focus on characters confronting a knowledge that has ultimately fated their path.[1] By the end of the first episode, we learn that our protagonists, Ray Velcoro, Ani Bezzerides, and Paul Woodrugh, are all in some way troubled by different types of *sexual* knowledge: Is Ray's son the product of a rape? What is the origin of Ani's uneasy relationship to sex and sex-work? And why is Paul such a reluctant lover to such a beautiful girlfriend? All this is set against the backdrop of a particularly sexual murder victim, while Lera Lynn's moody bar singer—effecting a tragic chorus—draws attention to how repressed sexual knowledge has left our protagonists living their "least favorite" lives. So, sex, and different types of sexual knowledge, are on the agenda, if not at the heart of season two's tragic plot. And, at first glance, Aristotle's (384–322 BCE) tragic formula seems to be in play: season two has a notoriously complex plot, with a narrative twist to reverse our protagonists' intentions.[2] But, where Aristotle identified the necessity of including "incidents arousing pity and fear" to bring about tragedy's famous *katharsis*, season two speaks more to Friedrich Nietzsche's (1844–1900) views on tragedy—specifically, his views of the ancient Greek dramatist Euripides (480–406 BCE).

True Detective and Philosophy: A Deeper Kind of Darkness, First Edition.
Edited by Jacob Graham and Tom Sparrow.
© 2018 John Wiley & Sons Ltd. Published 2018 by John Wiley & Sons Ltd.

Euripides, Nietzsche tells us, transformed tragedy into a lesser version of its former glory by bringing "the masses" onto the stage and entertaining their everyday troubles—what Nietzsche describes as a "victory of the individual phenomenon over the universal."[3] Where tragedy once focused on only the "grand and bold traits" of the human condition, Nietzsche says, Euripides focused on the moral concerns of the masses. And this is where it gets controversial. Against season two's backdrop of civic corruption—land-grabs and pork-barrels—the tragedy takes up a modern form of morality for the masses that creates a *barrier* to tragic wisdom: namely, feminist morality.

Back up, I hear you say. Feminism is a good thing; how does it undermine the experience of tragedy? It's a good question. First, let's start with Nietzsche's views on tragedy.

Attic Tragedy: "Sometimes Your Worst Self Is Your Best Self"

Above all, for Nietzsche, tragedy is *ethical*. The type that does it best? Attic tragedy of the fifth century BCE. Why? Because, Nietzsche tells us, it stages a "fearlessness in the face of the fearsome and questionable," making us confront the reality of our being in the world so we are better able to cope with it in the future.[4] That is, tragedy poses a question: Who are we as humans, and what are we capable of? What limits should we impose on ourselves, and when do we go too far with those limits? In season one, for instance, we confront something like the worst version of humanity in Errol Childress and the practices surrounding the mysterious Carcosa, but we're able to do it through the eyes of possibly our best self in Rustin Cohle. Sure, Rust admits to being one of the bad guys, but this is what makes him a better version of humanity: his ability to confront his worst self, and find a way to knit that knowledge into something meaningful—in a way that doesn't hurt others.

Season two, by contrast, is a monument to the fact that you can't simply *tell* tragic truisms, such as Frank Semyon's remark that "sometimes your worst self is your best self" ("Down Will Come"), and get tragedy. So how does it work? For Nietzsche, it's about the Greek gods Apollo and Dionysus, who inspire the artistic forms appearing across various historical epochs. Apollo, the god of light, inspires beautiful *form*, classical lines, and symmetry. He reveals the image and the individual—think epic Homeric poetry and blocks of marble chiseled away to reveal the perfect dimensions of the human body. Dionysus, on the other hand, is the god of ecstasy—of form*less* abandonment, eroticism, and what the French call *jouissance*, an excess of pleasure beyond normal limits. You're probably familiar with him as the god of wine and the sacred orgy, where, in the transgressing of social taboos, we return to a primal state of being. Dionysus inspires a loss of individuality in the orgiastic return to matter. For Nietzsche, ultimately, Dionysus is the god of music, rhythm, and dance, art in which the artists abandon themselves to *become* the art.

Great art, Nietzsche contends, needs both gods in harmony, because there's a terrifying violence to Dionysus: one can go *too* far in transgressive abandonment, as we saw when Rust returned to the drug world in "Who Goes There." When in excess, Apollo's emphasis on image can lead to *illusion* rather than representation. But together, Apollo veils the destructive quality of Dionysus, allowing us to glimpse our primal existence beneath our layers of civility. At best, then, tragedy speaks a Dionysian wisdom, the truth of our being in the world, mediated through Apollo's sage rationality. Nietzsche scholar Tim Themi summarizes tragedy as "lure[ing] us to face the difficulties of the human condition," to confront "the harshest, most amoral truths of our existence" that are "crucial for an informed ethics."[5]

Though not *billed* as tragedy, the first season of *True Detective* has plenty of these elements. In many ways, Rust's philosophical outlook establishes the Apollonian function of tragedy by providing a filter through which to confront the "difficulties of the human condition" expressed in the mysteries of Carcosa. This is important, because the Judeo-Christian morality of the bayou doesn't affirm Dionysian eroticism or confront the question of being. So Errol Childress' effort to come up with a more Dionysian religious meaning through the rituals of Carcosa, though horrific, is put into perspective through Rust's philosophy. His Nietzschean indictment of Christianity—"what's it say about life, hmm? You gotta get together, tell yourself stories that violate every law of the universe just to get through the goddamn day?"—shows us the more pervasive and no less depressing horror of an unquestioned life.

As with Attic tragedy, then, season one isn't a story with a tragic ending but one that forces a confrontation with our being in the world. Jacques Lacan (1901–1981)—the French Freud—says that in tragedy we learn "a little more about the deepest level" of ourselves than we "knew before."[6] But to do this effectively, Lacan suggests, the drama has to cross over or go beyond the limits of a little thing called "the good." Let me explain.

"The good" is the set of values we erect to channel our instinct for self-interest toward social harmony. Put crudely, instead of fighting and fucking all the time, we place taboos on sex and violence that form a limit between the social group—the *common* good—and our baser instincts. But sometimes the values of the good get out of hand. Remember when Rust tells Marty that, if a "common good" has to "make up fairy tales" about life then it's "not good for anyone"? He's talking through Nietzsche, but it's the same good Lacan wants us to *cross* in tragedy, because we need to transgress the limits of the good—go beyond the taboos that install it—to achieve tragic wisdom. We don't *discard* these taboos (or the good), but, for the duration of the drama and from the safety of our theater seat, we go beyond them to confront the Dionysian knowledge they hold in check.

Dionysian Wisdom or a Philosophy of the Good?

If we look at Ani's namesake, the heroine of Sophocles' tragedy *Antigone*, we get a reasonable idea of the good in question.[7] Antigone breaks the laws of the city that say she can't bury her brother's body because he's a traitor. She does it anyway, because blood is blood and she'd rather face the wrath of the city than the gods for not honoring the dead properly. *Antigone* is a confrontation between the civic law—Apollo's rational province, what's best for the city, for "the good of all"—and the archaic law of the gods with respect to life and death (Hades, Dionysus). The play asks us to contemplate: What happens when our investment in "the good of all" is taken *too* far? When the good becomes an inflated *ideal*, inflexible toward circumstance and Dionysian wisdom, it becomes the Good, capital G: a thing in itself, a restrictive, unbending ideal, rather than a moderating limit.

Antigone is considered just as rash and unbending as the civic Good in this case—the chorus initially judges her harshly—and she's buried alive as punishment. Here she dies by suicide, fearless in the face of the Good, and she is no one's victim. Her actions *cross* the limits of the Good, despite the deathly consequences, in what Lacan calls a "violent illumination," because her transgression inspires a thorough questioning of the Good, after which it can be restored in a more moderate mode.

Nietzsche thinks Euripides writes his plays under the influence of this Good—a social *ideal*—abandoning tragic Dionysian wisdom for a new morality developed by Euripides' friend Socrates (470–399 BCE), and later Plato (428–348 BCE) in his theory of forms. In Nietzsche's reading, Plato overvalues the *idea* of things above *actual*, material things, introducing a type of ideal Good that undervalues our earthly, material existence.[8] In Plato's *Symposium*, for example, "love" is valued as an ideal Good above a degraded material sexuality. In general, this seems unimportant, but, in terms of the tragic formula (and season two's focus on sexual knowledge), it matters. Showing "courage in the face of reality" denotes a strong "will-to-live" in a Dionysian tragedy, says Nietzsche. By contrast, Nietzsche thinks Plato shows cowardice in the face of reality and escapes it for ideals. Lacan agrees and thinks this is why tragedy needs to cross or transgress the ideals overinvested in the Good—however momentarily—so as to arrive at Dionysian truths of our being.

But this is no easy feat. While, as Lacan puts it, "the voice of the hero trembles before nothing and especially not before the good of the other," *we* must overcome our "fear" or "pity" in order to confront the wisdom revealed through this crossing.[9] While Aristotle saw tragedy as arousing pity and fear to cathartically purge it, in *The Will to Power* Nietzsche notes that tragedy is an art that requires that we overcome pity and fear to strengthen our personal ethics.[10] When head of HBO programming Michael Lombardo said that season one explored "the darkness in men and women" but without "judging it," he neatly summed up Nietzsche and Lacan's views on tragedy, where morality doesn't stop us from confronting the fearsome and the questionable.[11] But what about season two?

"Sometimes Your Worse Self Is" Just … Worse

In a reversal of season one, which questions the Good, season two follows Euripides in reducing Apollo and Dionysus to "good" and "evil" forces. Nietzsche identifies in Christian morality (which he calls "Platonism for the masses")[12] an emphasis on an inflated, moral Good that turns us against our instincts—against life—and labels them "vice."[13] This is what we get in season two. In season one, the mysteries of Carcosa give us this distortion of Dionysus as evil. Because the practices surrounding Carcosa are born from the Tuttle Christian dynasty, the erotic aspects of these practices express a return of what the church has repressed. In Freudian terms, when something is repressed, it will return to the surface in distorted form, so the rituals of Carcosa animate Dionysus in the form of the devil—barbaric and destructive rather than erotically life affirming. But in season two, not only is there no affirmation of sex, but also we don't really *investigate* it either: sex is only on the margins of the criminal activity, as an evil associated with corruption.

The catalyst for the drama is, of course, the murder of a guy (Ben Caspere) killed for liking "young trim"; his eyes are destroyed by acid and his sexual organs are blown off at close range. Sounds very Oedipal, but what it says about sexuality is more a moral statement about sexual enjoyment. The tragedy is that Caspere has already internalized this morality, his "tremendous shame and self-loathing" sending him to psychotherapy ("Night Finds You"). Under this moral Good, a specific type of sexual knowledge becomes hubristic for each of our protagonists—the thing that brings about their downfall. Woodrugh experiences so much shame over his sexuality that he ends up murdered, and both Ani and Ray murder people in reaction to the traumatic impact of sexual knowledge in their past. Additionally, for Ani, this traumatic past conflicts with her current sexual enjoyment in ways she doesn't know how to reconcile. In this Euripidean frame, where Apollo has become an *ideal* Good and there is little affirmation of

Dionysus—or our material and physiological instincts, drives, and desires—we all suffer *with* our protagonists. For, unlike season one, with its philosophical interrogation of Judeo-Christian morality, season two has no meta-philosophical framing, no Rust, to put this ideal Good into perspective.

And this is where the tragedy of season two perplexes. There's no shortage of sex, but it's mostly alluded to off screen: we're not privy to any eroticism. Even Ani and Ray's coupling—one of the more extensive sex scenes or, at least, one of significance—is a little ho-hum in its tastefully edited modesty. There's no shortage of violence in season two either, yet, as a substitute for repressed Dionysian eroticism, it too feels banal. There's nothing as barbarically transgressive as the practices of Carcosa because, in season two, the repressed violence of Dionysus returns over the issue of money. In Lacanian terms, the taboos imposed by the Good have diverted everyone's energies in the city of Vinci toward the *service* of goods—the accumulation of wealth, which is another kind of violence enforcing taboos on our instinctual life (in "Omega Station," Ani says money is "paid for in blood").[14] Even in the final episodes, when Ani confronts her repressed past at the Full Moon orgy and Athena warns her "you get on that bus and it's fuck or run," what does Ani do? The painfully repressed returns and she kills a guy, then runs. It's exactly what Nietzsche finds in Euripides' *The Bacchae*, where Dionysus returns to "destroy those who denied him" in "a return of the repressed *as* repressed."[15]

So why stage a tragedy with only a repressed Dionysus in it? Are we not adults? Is this not HBO? This is where feminism comes in, becoming season two's contemporary mode of the Good.

A "Good Woman" to "Mitigate Our Baser Tendencies"?

Season two animates some of the consequences of feminist logic where it aims at a common good—a moral guide for the masses—but becomes excessive and subsequently the Good that forms a barrier to tragic wisdom. Ani's conflicts about sex, for example, seem (partially) tied up in a feminist logic that purifies women's sexuality, identifying them as victims of male desires such that they become innocent of any desire or, at least, their desires are imagined wholly Good by contrast. In the first episode, Ani confronts her sister Athena over her web-cam activities, animating Ani's feminist position where it conflicts with post-feminist attitudes. Athena might be considered post-feminist in the sense that, though embracing *aspects* of feminism, she moves beyond its collective second-wave concerns to celebrate her desirability to men and self-interest in the form of sex-work, which, for feminist Ani, is "not right, it's not *healthy*."[16]

In the same episode, Eliot Bezzerides deconstructs Ani's feminist persona with a mix of Sigmund Freud (1856–1939) and Nietzsche that shows us the origin of Ani's feminism in her personal resentment toward her father. Eliot charges Ani with being "angry at the whole world—and men in particular—for a false sense of entitlement for something you never received," alluding to Freud's theory of penis envy where, in his clinic, Freud found that some girls developed a personality structured around resentment and envy after discovering they didn't have a penis.[17] The symbolism of Ani's "robot dick" e-cigarette and knife "equalizers" suggest that Eliot's analysis might be right. For, though most feminists reject Freud's theory, some see penis envy as a legitimate response to the discovery of anatomical differences: where these differences carry *symbolic* statuses and have social effects, resentment is understandable.[18] But Ani's resentment at not being physically equivalent to a man—the "difference between the sexes is that one of them can kill the other with their bare hands" ("Night Finds You")—speaks of the material reality to her difference and carries a certain Nietzschean *ressentiment*.

In *On the Genealogy of Morals*, Nietzsche develops the term *ressentiment* to describe resentment acted out in a type of revenge against an imagined oppressor.[19] Ani's *ressentiment* toward her father is partially due to his failure to protect her, but it also locates him as her oppressor, as if he somehow had a role in the random allotment of Ani's sex. Here, Ani follows Nietzsche's description of Plato's ideal Good: she reacts against material reality (being born female) by escaping into *ideals*, acted out via police work that Eliot further suggests isn't even something she enjoys, just "a reflexive urge towards authority" ("The Western Book of the Dead"). And where Eliot suggests that Ani's "entire personality is an extended criticism of" his values ("The Western Book of the Dead")—especially where he rejects universality for individual "truths"—we see how her critique of her father becomes conflated with the feminist critique of patriarchy—and takes on the feminist Good of the masses—precisely what she needs to *cross*, or go beyond, to confront Dionysian wisdom.

Feminism as the Good

There's no doubt that the idea of crossing feminist values, in general, is hard to swallow. Feminism's intellectual roots are in the Enlightenment, and who's going to argue with the age of reason, its ideas about universal freedom and human rights? After sixty-odd years of second-wave feminism in the West, it's *de rigueur* to graduate from your liberal arts college with a working knowledge of feminist film theory and the dehumanizing form of sexual objectification that is "the male gaze." But feminist principles are taken too far in season two and become the Good that should be crossed where it limits tragic wisdom. For it's not just Ani speaking from a position of the feminist Good.

For example, you might have thought it odd in the first episode when reformed gangster Frank tells Ray to find himself a "good woman" to "mitigate" his baser instincts, but it's a reminder of how feminism, heir to Immanuel Kant's (1724–1804) moral philosophy, becomes the Good. Kant felt that our humanness—our dignity—distinguishes us from the animal kingdom and that sexual activity outside monogamous marriage reduces us to animals, where we lose our special dignity and become degraded as "objects" or "instruments" of another's sexual appetite.[20] This sounds a lot like Ani in episode seven, when she tells Vera, "maybe you were put on earth for more than fucking," and it also speaks to Ani's problem not with fucking but with being an object of desire. In sex-work, certainly, we *do* reduce each other to instruments of sexual appetite, but it doesn't follow that we always lose dignity when consenting to be an object for someone else. Vera is pretty pissed at being "rescued" from sex-work because the money provides a comfortable life—an arguably no less dignified life than that of those who pay for her services because, as Vera exclaims, "*everything* is fucking." The pursuit of wealth—all the land-grabs and pork-barrels—sees Dionysus return as repressed in the brutally clinical violence of money. Everyone is getting metaphorically fucked over for money and power, so one may as well fuck literally *for* money, and perhaps enjoy some Dionysian transgression.

Athena also promises a more liberal post-feminist attitude—"not everybody has a problem with sex"—before reaffirming sex-work as degrading by justifying web-camming as "performance" and balking at the Full Moon parties, "the real hooking" ("Down Will Come"). Though Ani obviously has a sex life, she can only admit to enjoying it (and in "Other Lives" big, thick dicks you "have trouble handcuffing") through sarcastic negation, while the sex itself remains off screen, as if irrelevant to her story or as if such depictions would *degrade* her through our objectifying gaze and lessen her heroism.

Is Athena Right? Is This Just "My Fucking Problem?"

To be sure, the good (small "g") is something we need. But putting a taboo on sex and violence to create social harmony doesn't get *rid* of sex and violence; it just ignores or represses it (where it's all the more fascinating) so that, when it does reemerge, we don't know what to do with it—the mysteries of Carcosa are a case in point. It's under the influence of the feminist Good that season two represses or, at best, ignores sexual reality so as, ironically, *not* to objectify and degrade its protagonists. But with what effect?

Compare season one's depiction of down-and-out sex-workers with the no-holes-barred eroticism of Marty's sexual trysts. All around the bayou, lackluster sex-workers appear pitiable. Like Marty, we look to the Good to save them, condemning the sexual appetite that fuels the sex industry that degrades them. By contrast, when Beth seduces Marty out of his commitment to Maggie in "Haunted Houses," it isn't just a gratuitous "tits and ass" shot: it shows us something about sex important for our questioning of the Good and the limit Christian morality (its insistence on marital monogamy) imposes on sexuality. We see the power of the sexual drive and its fascination in Beth's eroticism. It's what Lacan describes as the "function of the beautiful" in tragedy. It draws us closer to the reality of our sexual drives, our desire—however dangerous to the status quo—so we can fashion a more honest and informed way of incorporating it into our lives.

The lure of beauty gets us closer to Dionysian truth, but in the first episode of season two, when the beautiful Emily tries to seduce Woodrugh (virtually the only scene with comparable eroticism to season one), she is shot down, and so are we. Dionysian knowledge is repressed here—we don't get any from Woodrugh's homosexual encounters either—and we're left feeling as if Emily shouldn't have objectified herself. We feel the need to reassert the feminist Good that might have saved her the indignity.

The Crossing of the Good

You might be questioning *my* morality right now, and I don't want to suggest we abandon morality or the good in general. But in tragedy? If we want Dionysian wisdom or enlightenment about the human condition, we need to be willing to question ideals, however noble—however good. We need to be willing to transgress or go beyond the limits of the good that hold us all in check. The problem with feminism as the Good is that, in a drama about sexuality, we were asked to avert our eyes. In episode seven, Eliot tells Ani she is innocent, but of what? Murder? A personality based on an imaginary revenge against "men in general" if not Eliot in particular? Ani's innocence is idealism, an Apollonian *illusion* of the feminist Good that, if properly questioned, might have revealed something about its limits. We know that Ani is a victim (of childhood abduction, at least), but, as a victim according to the feminist Good, she is unaccountable. Though in episode seven she admits to "waiting my whole life" to confront and kill a man, and maybe "even went looking," Ani's actions or *reactions* (a personality based on imaginary revenge that results in murder) don't question the feminist Good that makes her innocent, fearsome though it may be.

There's no doubt that crossing the limits of the Good is easier said than done. Getting too close to the Dionysian thing, Lacan tells us, can inspire *anguish*, a sense of anxiety as we transgress moral taboos installed to produce social harmony.[21] In "Haunted Houses," for example, monogamy overinvested as a moral Good is questioned when Maggie seduces Rust into a primal fuck so Marty might finally leave her. It's a graphic scene, as distressing as it is brutally erotic. Our enjoyment is mixed with anguish, not because Maggie is objectified but because we feel the anguish of transgression, of crossing a limit, of getting too close to the Dionysian thing, and its consequences.

Is Ani's reconciling of her repressed sexual knowledge properly transgressive? Properly tragic? One senses that the Full Moon orgy is supposed to shock: a confrontation with the knowledge that troubles her. It's given an *Eyes Wide Shut* quality, but, as a backdrop to civic corruption, there's not much about consensual adults engaging in sexual commerce to induce anguish. As a result, we don't confront the "harshest, most amoral truths" of our sexuality at the orgy but see it through Ani's eyes, literally seeing her abductor in the faces of rich old men—the patriarchy—degrading Good women with their baser instincts. And when Ani admits her repressed truth in "Omega Station"—she enjoyed being the object of desire ("he told me I was pretty" and "I felt proud")—we're made to feel for her as a *victim*, not a heroine, because she feels "sick"—*degraded*—by her pride.

Ani admits she's been "unfair" to people, and we'd be unfair to Ani if this were real life. But in tragedy? There's no Dionysian wisdom when our protagonist runs from her truth into ideals. Like Euripidean tragedy, where the hero gets a well-earned reward, Ani and Jordan walk into the night with Ray's baby in what seems more a victory for *Thelma & Louise* fans than anything tragic. The ethics of sexuality are left underexplored and *we* are left with the symptoms: the reality of *not* confronting their origin and of accepting the prevailing version of the Good that governs our social group (in this least favorite season, feminism), whose virtuous are left holding the baby.

Notes

1. Rich Cohen, "Can Nic Pizzolatto, *True Detective*'s Uncompromising Auteur, Do It All Again?" *Vanity Fair*, June 30, 2015. http://www.vanityfair.com/hollywood/2015/06/nic-pizzolatto-true-detective-season-2-better-than-season-1.

2. Aristotle, *Poetics* (Project Gutenberg, 2007). http://www.gutenberg.org/ebooks/20685.

3. See Friedrich Nietzsche, *The Birth of Tragedy: Out of the Spirit of Music*, trans. Shaun Whiteside, ed. Michael Tanner (London: Penguin, 2003), 80–84.

4. Friedrich Nietzsche, *Twilight of the Idols*, trans. R. Hollingdale (London: Penguin, 1990), IX: 24; see also Tim Themi, "Bataille and the Erotics of the Real," *Parrhesia* 24 (2015): 287.
5. Without mincing words, this essay owes a lot to Tim Themi's *Lacan's Ethics and Nietzsche's Critique of Platonism* (Albany: SUNY Press, 2014); quotation at page 3.
6. Jacques Lacan, *The Seminar of Jacques Lacan, Book VII: The Ethics of Psychoanalysis 1959–1960*, trans. D. Porter (London: Routledge, 1997), 323.
7. Sophocles, *The Three Theban Plays: Antigone, Oedipus the King, Oedipus at Colonus*, trans. Robert Fagles (New York: Penguin, 1984).
8. Nietzsche, *Twilight of the Idols*, 117.
9. Lacan, *Seminar VII*, 323.
10. Friedrich Nietzsche, *The Will to Power* (2 vols.), ed. Oscar Levy, trans. Anthony Ludovici (Digireads.com Publishing, 2010), 319.
11. Lacey Rose, "*True Detective*'s Nic Pizzolatto on Season 2, 'Stupid Criticism' and Rumors of On-Set Drama," *The Hollywood Reporter*, August 15 (2014).
12. Friedrich Nietzsche, *Beyond Good and Evil: Prelude to a Philosophy of the Future*, trans. Walter Kaufmann (New York: Vintage Books, 1989), 2.
13. Themi, *Lacan's Ethics*, 66.
14. See Lacan, *Seminar VII*, 324; Themi, "Bataille and the Erotics of the Real," 326.
15. Themi, "Bataille and the Erotics of the Real," 287.
16. See Horbury, *Post-feminist Impasses in Popular Heroine Television: The Persephone Complex* (Houndmills: Palgrave Macmillan, 2015).
17. See Freud's "On the Sexual Theories of Children," in *The Standard Edition of the Complete Psychological Works of Sigmund Freud, Volume IX (1906–1908)*, ed. James Strachey (London: Vintage Books, 2001).
18. Lisa Appignanesi and John Forrester, *Freud's Women* (New York: Other Press, 2000), 458.
19. Nietzsche, Friedrich, *On the Genealogy of Morals and Ecce Homo*, trans. Walter Kaufmann and R. J. Hollingdale (New York: Vintage Books, 1989), 36.
20. Immanuel Kant, *The Metaphysics of Morals* (Cambridge: Cambridge University Press, 1996).
21. See Jacques Lacan, *The Seminar of Jacques Lacan, Book X: Anxiety*, trans. A. R. Price (Cambridge: Polity, 2014).

15

The Noir Detective and the City

Chuck Ward

What the fuck is Vinci?
A city, supposedly.
　　　　　—Elvis Ilinca and Ray Velcoro in "The Western
　　　　　　　　　　　　　　　　Book of the Dead"

This place is built on a co-dependency of interests.
　　　　　—Frank Semyon in "The Western Book of the Dead"

Hard-boiled detectives have always had a peculiar relationship to their city. From the earliest examples of Philip Marlowe in Los Angeles or Sam Spade in San Francisco to more recent cases such as V. I. Warshawski in Chicago or Héctor Belascoran Shane in Mexico City, the noir detective is deeply connected to the city.

The second season of *True Detective* bears many marks of a classic urban-noir crime drama. The urban landscape is no mere setting for the action, nor is it simply an environment occupied by the detective. The city is a central character of the narrative. And the relationship between the detectives and the city is one of the crucial elements of the story. This is most obvious in the case of Vinci Detective Ray Velcoro, and apparent to a lesser degree in the cases of Ani Bezzerides and Paul Woodrugh.

This chapter examines the philosophical aspect of the relationship between the detective and the city, comparing it to a classical

True Detective and Philosophy: A Deeper Kind of Darkness, First Edition.
Edited by Jacob Graham and Tom Sparrow.
© 2018 John Wiley & Sons Ltd. Published 2018 by John Wiley & Sons Ltd.

view of the relationship between philosophy and the city, presented by Plato over two millennia ago in his dialogues *Apology* and *The Republic*. The *Apology* tells the story of Socrates on trial. In defending himself, Socrates explains the role of the philosopher in the city. There are some parallels between Socrates and the noir detective on this score, but there are some stark differences as well. These divergences highlight ways in which Plato's idealism contrasts with the more cynical, modern outlook of the noir genre overall and *True Detective* in particular. This is not to say that Plato failed to recognize the darker aspects of human beings and human society. This can be seen in his comparison between cities and the structure of our souls in his *Republic*. This feature of Plato's philosophy is also reflected in *True Detective*.

It may seem weird to compare messed-up characters such as Velcoro, Bezzerides, and Woodrugh from *True Detective* to philosophers such as Socrates. The old philosopher may be a pretty eccentric character, but he is usually thought of as virtuous and wise. In contrast, our detectives struggle with personal demons. While they may have certain heroic or virtuous qualities, these are more than balanced by weaknesses and flaws. Velcoro in particular has vices galore: alcohol, drugs, graft, lack of self-control. Nevertheless, the comparison can be helpful in gaining insight into some aspects of the human condition and modern life. It isn't the personality or moral character of Socrates that resembles the detectives, mind you. There is, rather, an analogy in the role Socrates and the detectives play in society. Moreover, the comparison is not all on the positive side. The differences between Socrates and the detectives are important, too.

Philosophy and the City

Plato (428–348 BCE) lived in the city of Athens, and yes, the city is indeed named for the goddess Athena, namesake of Ani Bezzerides' sister in *True Detective*. Athens was the most politically, economically, and culturally important city in the Greek world during Plato's lifetime. It was in Athens that the Greek theatrical tradition found its most celebrated practitioners, in the likes of Aeschylus (525–456 BCE) and Sophocles (470–399 BCE). The latter wrote the great tragedy *Antigone*, about the daughter of Oedipus and namesake of detective Bezzerides. Ancient Athens was also home to many of the great philosophers of the era. Plato's mentor Socrates was a new kind of philosopher in his day. At a certain point in his life, he decided that the god Apollo had charged him with the task of drawing his fellow Athenians into philosophical self-examination. So Socrates went around questioning people about their beliefs and their values. When they answered, he led them through rigorous critical appraisals of their positions. Often people would come out looking either shallow or dumb. Well, not so much dumb as deluded. Socrates showed them that their confident convictions often had no real basis. They just didn't know what they were talking about. They took too much for granted. According to Socrates, the key to improving themselves as persons, and to improving their collective lives as citizens, was to force themselves to critically examine their lives and their beliefs. "The unexamined life is not worth living," says Socrates in the *Apology*.[1]

Socrates was not a popular person. People found his behavior annoying, and they did not like the way he pestered them into questioning things they were comfortable with. They were often embarrassed by the outcome. Even worse, they found his willingness to criticize the common values and beliefs of society dangerous. Eventually he was put on trial for corrupting the youth and teaching inappropriate religious views (in the opinion of common Athenians). He was convicted and put to death. In those days, anyway, philosophy was about as dangerous as challenging the corrupt system in Vinci.

Plato wrote about the trial in the *Apology* (the Greek word *apologia* does not refer to saying sorry—it actually means "defense"). In the process of defending himself, Socrates presents a philosophy of the city. For Socrates, philosophy is primarily an anthropology, a moral science of the person. But the person is not just the individual man or woman. People, for Socrates and the Greeks generally, are essentially social beings. So the science of the person is analogous to the science of society. Socrates presents a view of the city as being like a person in some ways. In Plato's *Republic*, also starring Socrates, we are told that the city can be virtuous or wise. Or the city can lack these qualities, like the city of Vinci does.

In the *Apology*, Socrates claims that the god Apollo has attached him to the city. In arguing against his own execution, he says:

> Indeed, men of Athens, I am far from making a defense now on my own behalf, as might be thought, but on yours, to prevent you from wrongdoing by mistreating the god's gift to you by condemning me; for if you kill me you will not easily find another like me. I was attached to this city by the god—though it seems a ridiculous thing to say—as upon a great and noble horse which was somewhat sluggish because of its size and needed to be stirred up by a kind of gadfly.[2]

Modest fellow, isn't he? But this gadfly metaphor is a central feature of Socrates' philosophy of the city. It is really an account of the relationship between the philosopher and the city. What exactly is the job of this "gadfly"? Socrates explains:

> I shall not cease to practice philosophy, to exhort you and in my usual way to point out to any one of you whom I happen to meet: Good sir, you are an Athenian, a citizen of the greatest city with the greatest reputation for both wisdom and power; are you not ashamed of your eagerness to possess as much wealth, reputation, and honors as possible, while you do not care for nor give thought to wisdom or truth, or the best possible state of your soul?[3]

The philosopher is there to help his fellow citizens improve their souls. He helps them set their souls in order and orient their lives toward wisdom and virtue. In doing so he helps to move the city itself toward a state of order and justice.

This seems awfully idealistic. On the other hand, people do sometimes strive to become better, though it is not always possible without some kind of social support. I am reminded of Frank Semyon, the gangster character in the second season of *True Detective* (he hates it when people call him a gangster). He certainly is a ruthless and nasty fellow, but he yearns to live a more legitimate life. Ultimately he fails in this aim. Perhaps he could have benefited from knowing Socrates.

Thus the philosopher does not just happen to live in the city, wandering around annoying people. The philosopher is an integral and necessary part of the city. He belongs to the city as an organ belongs to an organism. He is, so to speak, the moral organ of the community. Yet people tend to marginalize Socrates (and philosophy in general) by dismissing him as engaged in pointless semantic games that have no relevance to "real life." Maybe this is because they misunderstand philosophy and its benefits. Socrates suggested it is because they want to avoid giving an account of themselves. Philosophy makes us nervous, but, if Socrates is right, it can also help us to live better lives. So Socrates is both at the center of the (moral) life of the city and at the margins of the society at the same time.

The Dark City of the Detective

The urban setting is a crucial element in the social world of noir. The hard-boiled cop or private eye works in a world of complex social, class, racial, and gender relations that must be negotiated and investigated in order for the detective to achieve their aim. Not everything is open to view. The detective must patrol dark streets and alleyways and visit underground establishments. People's identities and relationships are often concealed. The detective must shine a light in these dark places in order to resolve the mystery at hand. The characters in *True Detective* live in this milieu.

Like Socratic philosophers, detectives operate at the center of the city and at its margins at the same time. This is perhaps most vividly illustrated in the geography of Ray Velcoro's home. He lives in the heart of Vinci, practically on the doorstep of its city offices—the core of a corrupt system. In many ways, Ray is part of the corruption that characterizes Vinci. However, in his capacity as a member of the team investigating the murder of Vinci city manager Ben Caspere, he is a disruptive force in that system. Ray, Ani, and Paul work to reveal the hidden connections within Vinci and across the state. Like Socrates, they function as mechanisms of self-examination for the city. It is worth mentioning that "the city" in this context is not just the municipality of Vinci. The social structure under scrutiny is the whole of the Los Angeles metropolis, represented perhaps by the images of the downtown LA skyline looming over the horizon. In fact, the system of relationships revealed by the work of the detectives spans the entire state of California.

The process is not entirely one of bringing things to light, however; it is not entirely one of revealing truth. The philosopher Gilles Deleuze (1925–1995) presents a helpful analysis of this issue in his essay "The Philosophy of Crime Novels,"[4] which looks at the difference between classic detective fiction and that of the noir persuasion. In the classic examples (Edgar Allan Poe, Arthur Conan Doyle, Agatha Christie, Émile Gaboriau, etc.), the detective is an agent of truth. The detective's activity is epistemic. He tracks down clues and carries out his ratiocination, thus revealing the truth and solving the mystery. The work is done, to use the words of Agatha Christie's famous Belgian detective Hercule Poirot, with "the little gray cells." This may lead to some restoration of order in society, since the criminal transgressor is usually identified, most often apprehended, and (at least implicitly) punished. This restoration of order is the outcome of serving a kind of abstract justice grounded in truth and knowledge.

By contrast, Deleuze suggests, the hard-boiled detective carries out a different sort of function. Their role *is* indeed related to the balance and order in the city. But the detective is an agent of action rather than truth. The agent effects change through action rather than ratiocination. "With *La Série Noire* [a series of crime fiction books from the Parisian publisher Gallimard, founded in 1945], we've become accustomed to the sort of cop who dives right in, come what may, regardless of the errors he may commit, but confident that something will emerge."[5] The detective does bring things to light, but by stirring things up: by producing a reaction on the part of the perpetrators and other players in the situation.

In "Church in Ruins," episode six of the second season of *True Detective*, Ani Bezzerides poses as a prostitute so that she can infiltrate a secret party, organized by Blake Churchman and Tony Chessani, to entertain powerful businessmen and politicians. The detectives do not know what they will find or find out at the party. Ani just goes in and improvises. The things that transpire at the party, and the documents found there by Velcoro and Woodrugh, set in motion the final chain of events for the season. The detectives do in fact shake things up, forcing the hand of the various players. These noir detectives are agents of action as much as or more than minds sifting evidence and making inferences. They employ their bodies by physically intervening, thus revealing the tangle of power relations that is steering the fates of the exploited and the victims of the crimes under investigation.

The outcome, while it may be some version of justice, is not a perfect justice grounded on a full disclosure of the truth. Rather, on Deleuze's suggestion, these narratives offer "a process of resolution that allows a society, at the limits of cynicism, to hide what it wants to hide, reveal what it wants to reveal."[6] Deleuze calls this feature of society "the power of falsehood."

The noir genre, *True Detective* included, presents a cynical view of modern society. The deeper the detectives dig, the more disturbing things appear. Part of what their investigations reveal is the degree to which the detectives, the victims of the crimes, and indeed everyone is caught in the web of relations that constitutes the city. The frequent shots of the tangled freeway interchanges, grim industrial infrastructure, and concrete canals present this cynical and dehumanizing reality in stark visual terms. While this system may inspire cynicism, it still represents some form of social order. It *is* the system in which people pursue their lives. Though it may well involve corruption and exploitation, some system of order is necessary. The plots of noir crime stories very often involve some disturbance to this order, some imbalance that threatens it. The investigations and actions of the detectives serve to restore this balance.

The result is not a Platonic order or justice. Nor is it a teleological move toward such an abstraction. The outcome is, rather, a restoration of an equilibrium between the various forces of life and corruption that sustain the city. Consider the conclusion of *True Detective* season two. Ray, Ani, and Paul do figure out who killed Caspere and how that murder fits into a jumble of criminal dealings and conspiracies. While some of the villains are killed or apprehended, others are free to continue their nefarious activities. The power structures that breed and support exploitation, crime, and corruption are as strong as ever. The detective remains cynical even at the conclusion of a case. This kind of "resolution" is typical in the genre. At the end of the iconic noir novel *The Big Sleep*, detective Philip Marlowe broods that the only permanent relief is "the big sleep" of death.[7]

The city, then, is not simply the setting of the drama. The city *is* this system of relations that constitutes the potential for transgression, compensation, and restoration of equilibrium. The system contains, as part of its constitutive elements, the dark alleys and darker arrangements between powerbrokers of the criminal and official sort. This system makes possible detectives themselves, their lives and their cynical outlook. Their actions reveal its inner workings and thus perturb the normal operation of the "power of falsehood." And yet, while detectives seem to be "battling" the injustices of that system, their actions do not transform it. In reality they are playing a part in the system itself.

The City Inside

This internal irony at the heart of the noir detective as a type can be compared to the case of the Socratic philosopher discussed at the start of this essay. The analogy is not precise. It has already been emphasized that, in the case of the hard-boiled detective, the investigation is not a matter of ratiocination—not a matter of an epistemic process leading to truth and ideal justice. The engine of the detective's investigation is, in a sense, brute action. However, there is a significant feature they share. The methods of the philosopher and the methods of the detective both serve the aim of self-examination. The city and its citizens are made to look at themselves as they are. Notice that it is not only the city that is under investigation. The individual person is the subject of the examination as well. This includes the detective. So the examination operates on two levels.

In his dialogue *The Republic*, Plato presents a comparison between the person and the city. There is an analogy between the social and political structure of the city on the one hand and the structure of the individual psyche or soul on the other hand. The city, he said, is made up of rulers (political officials), guardians (police and military), and producers (workers). A just city is one where these three political classes are in a harmonious relationship. For this to come about, each class must perform its function without interference from the other groups. The rulers should judge and legislate on purely rational and impartial grounds. They are not supposed to engage in commerce for the purpose of accumulating wealth, since that is the function of the producers. They certainly aren't supposed to use their political authority to further their own material interests or those of their friends and allies. The society portrayed in *True Detective* is the antithesis of this ideal of justice that Plato describes. The political bosses in Vinci are in league with corporate and underworld figures. They use their position and authority to enrich themselves at the expense of the citizens of California. The scenes of convoluted urban infrastructure could well represent the tangled relations between the classes in the city.

Consider the scenes in the opening credits sequence of the *True Detective* episodes in season two. The images of the urban landscape are superimposed on silhouettes of human figures, usually heads. Most often these are images of the detectives and other characters from the series. As noted earlier, these images of the bleak urban infrastructure represent the tangled structures and relations of the corrupt society. Now it seems that this condition is mirrored in the heads of individuals.

According to Plato, there is indeed a parallel structure in the city and in the person. Like the city, the individual has a tripartite structure. Each soul has a rational part (intellect), a spirited part (passions), and an appetitive part (appetites or desires). Each part has its proper role in the psychic life of the person. In the just and healthy person, decisions and judgments are made by the rational part. Desires and passions are there to provide motivation, drive, and intensity. So long as they do not interfere with the operation of reason in making judgments, the soul is well ordered and harmonious. Plato associates the just, well-ordered soul with philosophers. He considered philosophers, understood in this way, as "true rulers." This is what lies behind his infamous idea of the Philosopher King.

The characters in *True Detective* are not philosophers but realistic people. In actual human beings, passions and desires can get the better of us. They can gain control over executive functions. Plato describes a range of less healthy states of the soul in which the three parts of the soul are not engaged in harmonious cooperation. Instead, the soul is in varying degrees of turmoil and internal conflict. All three of the detectives exhibit some version of this condition. The turmoil going on in Velcoro is almost unbearable. His intense love for his son and his desire to maintain a strong relationship with him are tangled up with his doubt, his guilt, and his anger over the events around his son's conception. These issues have such a grip on his mind that he repeatedly makes disastrous decisions. The long history of these struggles and decisions leads Ray to the place he occupies in the narrative. Nominally he is a cop, charged with fighting crime and protecting the public. In reality, he is an agent working to protect the corrupt cabal of the Vinci city officials and their underworld allies. One example of this is his assault on the newspaper reporter writing stories about the state investigation of Vinci. Even as Ray collaborates with Bezzerides and Woodrugh to find Caspere's killer, he colludes with corrupt Vinci officials and with Frank Semyon to conceal their involvement in various conspiracies. Ray's actions reveal a tangle of conflicting aims, a web of contention reflected in Ray's internal turmoil. Even in "Omega Station," the final episode of season two, when the case has been more or less solved, when Velcoro and Ani seem to be moving toward rebuilding their lives and finding some measure of happiness, Ray's passions lead him astray.

The case of Detective Velcoro is an example of how *True Detective* season two illustrates aspects of Plato's philosophy. Plato had a degree of cynicism about his own society, to be sure. His ideas about the power of philosophy, though, carried a strong dose of idealism. Socrates' philosophical activities ensure some measure of self-examination, thus keeping the society from degenerating too far from a just condition. Plato himself, with his parallel models of the city and the soul, imagines how a truly just society is possible, at least in theory. *True Detective*, like all noir detective stories, presents a more deeply cynical view of society and human nature. Still, the Platonic themes of self-examination and parallels between the person and society are reflected in the narrative. Even if one is skeptical about Plato's idealistic socio-political theory, there are still things about his philosophy that can be used to gain insight into modern society and *True Detective*.

Notes

1. Plato, *Apology*, in *Five Dialogues*, second edition, trans. G. M. A. Grube, revised by John M. Cooper (Indianapolis: Hackett, 2002), 41.
2. Ibid., 35.

3. Ibid., 34.
4. Gilles Deleuze, "The Philosophy of Crime Novels," in *Desert Islands and Other Texts, 1953–1974*, ed. David Lapoujade, trans. Michael Taormina (Los Angeles: Semiotext(e), 2004).
5. Ibid., 83.
6. Ibid., 83.
7. Raymond Chandler, *The Big Sleep*, in *Chandler: Stories and Early Novels* (New York: Literary Classics of the United States, 1995), 763–764.

16

Cohle and Oedipus
The Return of the Noir Hero

Daniel Tutt

A bond of mutual dependence between two partners is at the heart of detective fiction. Typically, the relationship works, and the opposing personalities of the two partners strike a balance, enabling them to solve the crime. One detective tends to be cavalier and eccentric, following an almost supersensory intuition as they crack the case, while the other tends to be cautious and more responsible, providing balance to the eccentric vision of their partner. In the history of detective fiction literature, this structure of opposites began with Arthur Conan Doyle's Sherlock Holmes stories, where Watson functions as the rational and cool sounding board for the eccentric genius of Holmes. Importantly, Holmes unravels each crime by talking it out with Watson, and it is Watson who gives the sense to Holmes' vision. This structure of mutual dependence between the two detectives is central to the development of the truth of the crime in any given case. As Gilles Deleuze (1925–1995) notes in his study of detective fiction and philosophy, the structure of any detective story is at its core a philosophical pursuit:

> In the old conception of the detective novel, we would be shown a genius detective devoting the whole power of his mind to the search and discovery of the truth. The idea of truth in the classic detective novel was totally philosophical, that is, it was the product of the

True Detective and Philosophy: A Deeper Kind of Darkness, First Edition.
Edited by Jacob Graham and Tom Sparrow.
© 2018 John Wiley & Sons Ltd. Published 2018 by John Wiley & Sons Ltd.

effort and the operations of the mind. So it is that police investigation modeled itself on philosophical inquiry, and conversely, gave to philosophy an unusual object to elucidate: crime.[1]

Deleuze identifies two types of truth in the detective genre. The first is inductive, which is embodied by the Sherlock Holmes stories, where the detective induces the truth of the case by reading the signs that appear. This distinctly English school of the detective genre is associated with Thomas Hobbes (1588–1679). The second line of philosophical detection is the French school, embodied by the deductive method of René Descartes (1596–1650), which privileges reason over the senses. In this mode of truth seeking, the detective steps back from the world of sensuality, since the world of senses presents a fundamental falsehood, and the detective relies on their independent and detached reasoning to get to the truth of the crime.

How might we understand the first season of HBO's *True Detective* in light of these two models of truth? Before we answer this question, we must turn to the often-fraught relationship between the two detectives, Rust Cohle and Marty Hart.

The Lack of Cohle and Hart

The season begins with the two men reflecting on the seventeen-year-long murder investigation of prostitute Dora Lange and on several other unsolved crimes that brought both men on a harrowing and obsessive journey to solve them. Their reflections on video, in what appears to be the present day, reveal a relationship that is complicated and strangely tense from its beginning. There is a dark humor in the dialogue between Hart and Cohle that begins in the first episode, "The Long Bright Dark," as they drive through the barren southern wasteland and Cohle pontificates about his philosophical vision of pessimism.

The viewer quickly learns that Cohle is tormented by a long and brutal stint as an undercover drug informant, during which he became addicted to barbiturates. He still suffers from hallucinations and uncontrollable visions, which, as he confesses to Hart, "is not something that gets better" ("Form and Void"). Despite these erratic visions, Cohle possesses a great deal of inner control and commands a philosophical worldview that puts him completely at ease with his own lack.

The ways that Cohle and Hart relate to lack provide insight into how their oppositional relationship develops throughout the show. In the writing of the psychoanalyst and philosopher Jacques Lacan (1901–1981), lack is constitutive of the subject or self. To understand lack, Lacan asks that we begin with the image. In his famous "mirror stage" theory, Lacan claims that the human ego forms a narcissistic obsession with its own body as a whole image. The whole image of the ego is presented as the mirror that "gives the subject an imaginary mastery over his body, one which is premature in relation to a real mastery."[2]

When a young child sees its own image in a mirror, the child first sees itself as a whole body, but the field of desire, introduced by language and what Lacan calls "the field of the Other," compromises this original perception of wholeness, introducing lack. The child longs to inhabit the original sense of wholeness that the image of its body presents in the mirror, but desire introduces a series of holes into the body, preventing the child's attempt at mastery or wholeness. To inhabit this lack that desire brings about is painful and often fraught with difficulty. Lacan's notion of lack is not to be understood in a quantitative sense. It's not that one feels that one lacks proper achievements or longs for social recognition that one doesn't adequately receive. Rather, the subject continually confronts lack because the core of desire revolves around the question "What does the Other want from me?"—a demand that can never adequately be fulfilled.

By examining how both Cohle and Hart relate to this fundamental lack, we gain an insight into how their relationship develops a strange type of mutual dependence. Cohle basks in his own lack, appearing to be fully at peace with it, whereas Hart can't handle lack. As Hart's wife Maggie comments, "Cohle knows who he is," while Hart "doesn't know who he is" ("The Locked Room"). In the first three episodes, we are exposed to a version of Cohle in the 1990s that is completely at peace with his lack. His daughter was killed (because of his carelessness, no less) and he has undergone a traumatic stint as an undercover drug officer, witnessing the worst of humanity. But he maintains a strange peace with his own lack and with this trauma, which is reinforced by his philosophical view of humanity itself. In "The Long Bright Dark," Cohle expounds his philosophical worldview when he tells Hart: "We are things that labor under the illusion of having a self, that accretion of sensory experience of feelings, programmed with total assurance that we are each somebody, when in fact everybody's nobody."

While Cohle holds his philosophical beliefs with conviction, Hart is unreflective and lacks justification for his beliefs. Hart defers his beliefs with what social theorist Robert Pfaller calls "interpassivity."[3] Interpassivity is a theory that argues people defer or transfer their beliefs onto the Other, instead of believing on their own. Interpassivity is thus a type of avoidance of having to do the work of believing, whether that belief is in God, a higher power, or a philosophical system, opting instead to let the Other "do the believing for you."[4] In "The Locked Room," Hart and Cohle meet the charismatic evangelical pastor Joel Theriot and witness a passionate sermon in a tent full of his faithful followers. Cohle remarks that Theriot's evangelical congregants are sheepish and refuse to think for themselves, while Hart defends them as morally superior to Cohle's atheistic pessimism. Hart remarks, "at least some people still believe." Cohle responds with disdain for the evangelicals, claiming they blindly put their trust in an authority they haven't sufficiently questioned.

"You're Obsessed, Just Not with Your Work"

This world is a veil, and the face you wear is not your own.
—Preacher Joel Theriot

One of Sigmund Freud's (1856–1939) most important discoveries in psychoanalysis is the development of the neurotic subject, a set of nervous disorders that affect wide swaths of people in the modern world. The two most common forms of neurosis are hysteria and obsessional neurosis, but Freud identified neurotic symptoms as so common in modern humans that the line between what counts as normal and what counts as neurotic is constantly blurred. Hart clearly exhibits many of the classic signs of obsessional neurosis: an obsessional person may desire something, but, in order for them to desire it, it has to be an unattainable desire. Why is

Hart always tempted to cheat on his wife, despite the fact she is beautiful and loving? It's almost as if Hart does not know why he cheats. This uncertainty indicates that his cheating should not be read at the level of desire. It's not a matter of what the Other wants from him. Instead, a repetitive drive overcomes him.

For an obsessional person, the question that drives them is whether they deserve the object of desire or not. Lacan says that the object of desire is obtained by confronting the desire of the Other, and this exchange with the Other is what spooks an obsessional person. What spooks an obsessional person about the Other is the fear that they may be made into an object of the Other's desire. According to Freud, an obsessional person refuses to be an object of the Other because they fear feminization. As such, an obsessional person can only advance through a mask, because if they were recognized it would be shameful. The mask is what an obsessional person gives to himself or herself as a way to show who they are to the Other in order to avoid having to confront the lack at the core of their being.

Cohle basks in his lack. It shapes his eccentric philosophical musings, while Hart is made uncomfortable with Cohle's comfort with his own lack. The fact that the two partners deal with lack so differently eventually forces Cohle to quit the police force and give up on the case. As the season develops, the tension between Cohle and Hart culminates in the parking lot of the police station, where Cohle says to Hart, "you're obsessed, just not with your work." Not only is this statement deeply funny for its brutal honesty and for the quick-witted retort of Cohle but it also leaves the viewer wondering just what Hart is obsessed with. Hart has no great passions, no secret hobbies that he obsessively works on, and his job performance is largely functional. What makes Hart an asset to the management of the police force is that he's a straight shooter: clearheaded and responsible. He's not exceptional; he's not brilliant. Hart is Cohle's lifeline to the world of bureaucracy, which is why the culmination of tension erupts between both characters when Hart reminds Cohle of his constant support and defense of Cohle in the face of the other police officers who have cast Cohle as an eccentric. The mutuality of the two characters is thus revealed at this moment of tension. After it fizzles out, the two men are eventually able to regroup and solve the final case.

While Hart exhibits the behavior of an obsessional person, Cohle exhibits all the signs of a hysterical person. In hysteria, the dissatisfaction with the Other is structural. Each time the object of desire of the Other is to be obtained, the subject thinks: that's not it. The hysterical person is interested in the desire of the Other but content not to have that desire satisfied. This makes the hysterical person a privileged agent of ascertaining the truth. The question the hysterical person asks over and over to the Other is, "What kind of object am I for the Other?" Cohle is at ease with his lack, and his ease enables him to remain fixated on the desire of the Other. But he is never content with what he receives in return. This is precisely what makes Cohle the better detective, indeed the *true* detective. We can understand Cohle's special skill in getting convicts to confess their crimes in relation to this fundamental hysterical structure. Cohle is so effective in getting confessions because he never gets tangled in the Other's (criminal's) web of desire. This freedom from the desire of the Other makes Cohle objective and rational, able to get the truth out of anyone. But there is another reason why Cohle is able to get the truth out of the guilty conscience of the criminal. It is because Cohle himself is unable to experience guilt—the true sign of any noir hero.

Cohle and Oedipus: The Return of the Noir Hero

She spared me the sin of being a father.

—Cohle

In his reflections on detective novels, Deleuze argues that the core structure of the detective's search for truth follows an Oedipal trajectory. Sophocles' classic myth of Oedipus presents the basic structure of the detective genre. Oedipus' tragedy, that he killed his father and married his mother, is a story that shows that the parental function itself often does not function and instead fails. In a deleted scene from the first season, we discover that Cohle confesses his personal demons with having children. In an emotional conversation with his ex-girlfriend Lori, Cohle tells her that he made a "philosophical decision" not to become a father. "We've discussed this," he says. "As a subject, it's one that I've closed off to myself."[5] When Spencer tries to comfort Cohle in "The Secret Fate of All Life," he responds, "there's nothing to heal. I'll tell you, it's a philosophical decision." Like Oedipus, Cohle is concerned with reading his fate to the letter. Cohle develops a philosophy, specifically what is referred to as anti-natalism, or the belief that human beings should not procreate. Cohle's anti-natalism is based on the contingent accident of his daughter's death. Like Oedipus, Cohle fights to gain mastery over his destiny by forever denying the very role of father.

Lacan says that Oedipus was given the worst insult in this affair because he was not given the capacity to be guilty for his actions precisely because they were predetermined.[6] The words of the sphinx situated Oedipus' destiny in such a way that he was deprived of a destiny proper; he became an object of language because it was the words of the sphinx that set the course of his destiny. But, unlike Oedipus, Cohle is given a second chance in life after the tragic death of his daughter. This second chance results from becoming a true detective. We can understand Cohle's great inner struggle as a wrestling with his own destiny.

Like Oedipus, Cohle is a hero whose travails show that, in order to assume one's place in the world, one must make a sacrifice. The philosopher Georg Wilhelm Friedrich Hegel (1770–1831) remarks that the sign of any true subject is that they are prevented from experiencing guilt. This is the insult that Oedipus suffers: he is not permitted to be guilty, and this, as Hegel points out, is key to all heroes.[7] Oedipus does not kill his real father but rather kills the father function—he kills what Lacan called the symbolic father, a function that is destined to failure.[8]

The Lacanian philosopher Alenka Zupančič points out that Oedipus was the first noir hero precisely because in Oedipus the hero is also the villain—the two become indistinguishable. Cohle can read the signs all around him, but he has surpassed Oedipus. If Oedipus' problem, as Lacan notes, was that he was lacking in knowledge that knows itself, then Cohle has conquered this knowledge philosophically. He is aware that the father function is destined to a tragic impasse and he accepts it; he lets this impasse sit with him and finds a way to put it to work toward solving the case. Cohle's putting to work of his symptom is nothing less than what Lacan referred to as the work of the *sinthome*, where one develops a mastery over one's symptom, putting it to work in the labor of creation. Lacan pointed out how artists such as James Joyce overcame their psychosis through identification with their symptom.[9] Once Cohle is able to tie both forms of knowledge together—knowledge as truth (the case) and knowledge that knows itself—he is able to bring his symptom to a point of stability. The ending of season one represents the ending of Cohle's trajectory of a psychotic subject: he doesn't require another case to bring him peace of mind. What Cohle kills by the end of season one is the brutal reality that neither he, nor any father for that matter, can ever live up to the father function.

Notes

1. Gilles Deleuze, "The Philosophy of Crime Novels," in *Desert Islands and Other Texts, 1953–1974* (New York: Semiotexte, 2004), 81–82.
2. Jacques Lacan, *The Seminar of Jacques Lacan: Book I*, trans. John Forrester (New York: W. W. Norton and Co. 1993), 80.
3. Robert Pfaller, "Interpassivity and Misdemeanors: The Analysis of Ideology and the Zizekian Toolbox," *International Journal of Philosophy* 261 (2012/3), 261.
4. Ibid.
5. "True Detective Deleted Scene—Rust and Lori." *YouTube*, March 14, 2014. https://www.youtube.com/watch?v=89FObkqroZY.
6. Jacques Lacan, *Le Seminaire, livre VII: Le transfert* (Paris: Seuil, 1991), 354.
7. Georg Wilhelm Friedrich Hegel, *Aesthetics: Lectures on Fine Art* (Oxford: Clarendon Press, 1975), 360–361.
8. Jacques Lacan, *The Ethics of Psychoanalysis 1959–60*, trans. Dennis Porter (New York: W.W. Norton and Company, 1993), 309.
9. Jacques Lacan, *The Sinthome: The Seminar of Jacques Lacan, Book XXIII* (Cambridge: Polity Press, 2016), 141.

Part V

"TIME IS A FLAT CIRCLE"
Time in *True Detective*

17

Time Is a Flat Circle
Nietzsche's Concept of Eternal Recurrence[1]

Lawrence J. Hatab

I had not seen anything like it on television before. In *True Detective*, the character of Rust Cohle is remarkable in giving voice to pessimism: not in the ordinary sense of being a glass-half-empty type of person but in the full-blown philosophical sense that human consciousness is a "tragic misstep," that we are "programmed" to think there is meaning in our individual lives but that this is an illusion. Indeed, Cohle advises that we should "deny our programming, stop reproducing. Walk hand in hand into extinction."

A Purposeless Will at the Heart of Reality

It is jolting to hear this kind of thinking in a TV series, even on HBO (such a sentiment would not bode well for the future of entertainment). Right away I saw that Cohle's speech is drawn directly from the philosophy of Arthur Schopenhauer (1788–1860). For Schopenhauer, the ultimate nature of reality is the will, a blind assertive drive to live and satisfy desires. It is the drive that is primary, not any object of desire, or any individual agent of desire, or any satisfaction of desire. So the will never comes to rest in a state of fulfillment. All things exhibit the same basic force that finds no completion or ultimate satisfaction. Our sense of being individual selves striving for particular goals is only an "appearance" of a

True Detective and Philosophy: A Deeper Kind of Darkness, First Edition.
Edited by Jacob Graham and Tom Sparrow.
© 2018 John Wiley & Sons Ltd. Published 2018 by John Wiley & Sons Ltd.

single pointless driving energy within all things. The evidence for a purposeless will at the heart of reality is the constant reassertion of willing after any satisfied desire and the boredom we experience after achieving what we want. The surging of the will for individuals comes to a stop with death, but this is only an apparent cessation of the will because it continues to surge in all other beings.

Schopenhauer was a this-worldly thinker who did not believe in any reality beyond earthly life and who believed that a hard-eyed look at life reveals the absurdity of existence: we are naturally driven to satisfy our desires and to see life as purposeful, yet we often suffer from obstacles to desire, and, even when satisfied, desire continues to seek satisfaction—until all desires and purposes are canceled out by death. Suffering is therefore an inevitable part of life that cannot be overcome or fixed. We constantly seek what cannot be ultimately satisfied. Schopenhauer says that our response to this absurdity should be a denial of the will to whatever extent possible. In its strongest form, such a denial would be an ascetic renunciation of desires, especially the sexual drive to reproduce, which simply perpetuates the absurdity. For Schopenhauer, ascetic passivity rules out suicide (you must *will* to take your own life), but death is welcomed as a release from suffering and the futility of existence.

That, I think, is the philosophical source of Cohle's powerful speech in "The Long Bright Dark" about the tragic misstep of consciousness and the need to deny our programmed desires. In the series, it seems that Cohle's attitude may have stemmed from a terrible event in his life: his young daughter, while riding her tricycle, was run over and killed by a reckless driver. Surely something like that can affect a person's attitude toward life, but it should be said that, in Schopenhauer's philosophy, pessimism is a function of wisdom, not mood or terrible misfortune. Even if one did not experience deep trauma, that would not alter the global absurdity analyzed by Schopenhauer.

In the last episode of the first season, Cohle comes out of a coma and tells his partner, Hart, that he saw his daughter and father in his unconscious state. Then he says: "Once there was only dark. If you ask me, the light is winning." What is meant by the light winning? There is no overt retraction of his original pessimism, but the phrase seems to suggest a more positive outlook on life. In one sense it was satisfying to hear Cohle talk about the light, but dramatically speaking it seemed to come out of the blue. Was he simply getting over his grief-stricken attitude? Did he see or feel something that brought him away from pessimism? It is not clear. But I want to consider another speech by Cohle, which seems in line with Schopenhauer's pessimism but which also connects with another philosopher, Friedrich Nietzsche (1844–1900), whose core motivation was diagnosing pessimism as an illness and opting for the complete affirmation of earthly life.

The True Test of Life Affirmation

Cohle says: "Time is a flat circle. Everything we've ever done or will do, we're gonna do over and over and over and over again ... *forever*." This is Nietzsche's doctrine of eternal recurrence, as depicted in *The Gay Science* and *Thus Spoke Zarathustra*. It is clear that Cohle expresses this idea in a pessimistic mood and that it is meant to magnify the absurdity of life by declaring its endless repetition. I want to emphasize, however, that a pessimistic reading of eternal recurrence cannot be the last word in coming to terms with Nietzsche's offering. Whether this can have any bearing on Cohle's apparent change of heart is not evident to me, because he originally portrayed the repetition of life in a Schopenhauerian spirit.

Schopenhauer was an early influence on Nietzsche, and they agreed on certain basic things, including the primacy of a driving will, which generates perpetual conflict with no ultimate resolution and no salvation. They are on firm ground so far, because who can deny that life as we have it puts a tragic limit on all human interests and aspirations? No one gets out alive or unscathed. For both thinkers, this tragedy is the last word on existence, but they differ on whether life as we have it is worthwhile or meaningful. Schopenhauer's answer is "no" and Nietzsche wants to say "yes." Eternal recurrence, for Nietzsche, is a way to force attention on life exactly as it is, with no alternative, not even nothingness at the end of life, not even eternal novelty. If one could say "yes" to eternal recurrence—the endless repetition of life in exactly the same way—one could genuinely say "yes" to life as it is. It turns out that Schopenhauer said "no" to life specifically with regard to the possibility of its recurrence: "At the end of his life, no man, if he be sincere and at the same time in possession of his faculties, will ever wish to go through it again."[2] Who can blame him, at least regarding certain parts of life? For me, the eternal repetition of high school would be a nightmare.

Nevertheless, Nietzsche came to see Schopenhauer's pessimism as the secret code to the Western tradition.[3] Pessimism implies that life *should* support human interests in some fundamental way but *cannot*—why else turn away from life? Nietzsche applauded Schopenhauer's honest analysis of existence and his demolition of all "optimistic" doctrines that speak of salvation, transformation, or worldly progress. Nietzsche concluded that any such optimistic worldview is simply a *concealed* pessimism that seeks an alternative to life's tragic character, a "no" to life as it is. For instance, Christianity basically agrees with Schopenhauer about turning away from earthly life, but for the sake of an illusory salvation. According to Nietzsche, Schopenhauer was therefore able to spell out the pessimistic spirit of Western thought without concealment. Nietzsche diverged from Schopenhauer (and the tradition) in calling pessimism to account for the paradox of a living entity turning against life. If this life is all there is, how can existence be "absurd"? Perhaps life-denial is absurd. Nietzsche aims to find a way in which the tragic conditions of existence can be understood as *generating* meaning rather than canceling it out.

Eternal recurrence is announced in *The Gay Science* as a question posed to the reader:

> *The Greatest Weight.* What if some day or night a demon were to sneak after you in your loneliness and say to you: "This life as you now live it and have lived it, you will have to live once more and innumerable times more; and there will be nothing new in it, but every pain and every joy and every thought and sigh and everything immeasurably small or great in your life must return to you, all in the same succession and sequence—even this spider and this moonlight between the trees, and even this moment and I myself. The eternal hourglass of existence is turned over and over, and you with it, a speck of dust."
>
> Would you not throw yourself down and gnash your teeth and curse the demon who spoke thus? Or did you once experience a tremendous moment when you would have answered him: "You are a god, and never have I heard anything more godly." If this thought

were to gain possession of you, it would change you, as you are, or perhaps crush you. The question in each and every thing, "Do you want this again and innumerable times again?" would weigh upon your actions as the greatest weight. Or how well disposed would you have to become to yourself and to life to *desire nothing more* than this ultimate eternal confirmation and seal?[4]

Would such a prospect be a devastation or a joyous gift? Nietzsche's next book, *Thus Spoke Zarathustra*, provides a dramatic narrative depicting the task of life-affirmation in the face of eternal recurrence. Zarathustra comes to humanity in order to "redeem the earth," to speak for natural life against all life-denying doctrines.[5] Eternal recurrence is presented as the true test of life-affirmation, and Zarathustra goes through a deep trauma in confronting it. Saying "yes" to the repetition of life includes all the things we regret and despise, all the things that go against what we find meaningful. Zarathustra has to focus on what he most despises, the Small Man, who cannot rise to the challenge of life and affirm earthly existence, who dodges that task by dwelling in trivial pursuits, cheap satisfactions, and life-suppressing moral rules. With eternal recurrence, the Small Man will return again and again, forever. Zarathustra goes through gut-wrenching encounters with this terrible prospect, but in the end he comes to say "yes" to eternal recurrence, and thus to all of life, including the Small Man.

What is interesting here is that eternal recurrence as a test of life-affirmation *should* be a traumatic challenge because it forces attention on what goes *against* meaning in one's life. An easy "yes" to eternal repetition would not be an honest and direct assessment of tragic limits in existence. So the initial effect of eternal recurrence *should* border on the possibility of pessimism. But Nietzsche's philosophy aims to uncover an alternative to pessimism in terms of how things that go counter to meaning are actually implicated in meaning. The main avenue for this kind of thinking is his notion of will to power.

Finding Meaning in Conflict

Nietzsche's concept of will to power is often misunderstood. It is not restricted to physical force and it does not imply utter control. Will to power names a structured relation between conflicting forces, where meaning is found in *overcoming* a resisting or competing condition. Resistance is *required* for such a movement of overcoming, and so the elimination of a resistance would also negate the power to overcome and its meaning. This is why Nietzsche often speaks of needing opponents in order to shape one's own posture.[6] Think of the analogy of athletic competition, where contestants need each other for the opportunity to succeed and bring out their respective talents. A victory would mean nothing without a worthy opponent, and a weak opponent lessens the value of the win. The elimination or disabling of a competitor would therefore be self-defeating. Nietzsche's concept of will to power is built around a similar structure that connects meaning with opposition.

Will to power can manifest itself in any area of significance, in physical, practical, social, and cultural settings. That is why pacifism can be understood as a form of will to power, because it seeks to overcome human violence. In any case, Nietzsche is able to show how meaning needs countermeanings in order to *be* meaningful. Eternal recurrence presents a global view of how life can be truly affirmed by saying "yes" to all things, including things that oppose one's interests. But saying "yes" to eternal recurrence affirms opposing conditions *as* opposing conditions, which one must *oppose* to find one's own meaning. Life-affirmation, therefore, in the light of eternal recurrence, does not mean *approving* of everything that happens. One will eternally repeat one's opposition to counterconditions and eternally find meaning in that conflict. So Zarathustra will eternally oppose the Small Man, which is not endless dissatisfaction but the endless satisfaction of overcoming mediocrity.[7]

The "Lightening" of Cohle's Pessimism

Ultimately, the portrayal of eternal recurrence in *True Detective* is not in the spirit of Nietzsche's conception. It is more akin to Schopenhauer's response. Nietzsche finds a way to overcome pessimism by affirming life *because* of its tragic limits. How can this apply to Cohle's apparent change of heart at the end of the series? I don't know. On Nietzsche's terms, saying "yes" to life would entail the eternal repetition of his daughter's death. No small thing there. Pessimism would not be surprising in the face of such pain, not to mention the many vile acts that a homicide detective must regularly confront. The series certainly puts a spotlight on the darker side of human nature. But if the "lightening" of Cohle's pessimism stems from seeing his daughter and coming to believe in a supernatural dimension where she still exists—and television today seems awash in supernatural scripts—that would run counter to Nietzsche's vision of life.

Notes

1. An earlier version of this chapter originally appeared online at *The Critique*.
2. Arthur Schopenhauer, *The World as Will and Representation*, vol. 1, trans. E. F. J. Payne (New York: Dover, 1969), 324.
3. Friedrich Nietzsche, *The Gay Science*, trans. Walter Kaufmann (New York: Random House, 1974), sec. 357.
4. Ibid., sec. 341.
5. Friedrich Nietzsche, *Thus Spoke Zarathustra*, trans. Graham Parkes (New York: Oxford University Press, 2005).
6. See, for instance, Friedrich Nietzsche, "Morality as Anti-nature," in *Twilight of the Idols*, vol. 3, trans. Richard Polt (Indianapolis: Hackett, 1997), 26–27.
7. For a treatment of eternal recurrence in the context of Nietzsche's overall thought, see my *Nietzsche's Life Sentence: Coming to Terms with Eternal Recurrence* (New York: Routledge, 2005).

Eternal Recurrence and the Philosophy of the "Flat Circle"

Paul A. DiGeorgio

In *True Detective*, the description of time as a "flat circle" is one of the most mysterious aspects of the story. Time is described as somehow circular, cyclical, or eternal in no fewer than *five* distinct pieces of dialogue. In spite of this frequency, we are never told, in clear terms, what "time is a flat circle" means.

The first time we encounter the flat circle, Rust dismisses it, but all the way to the end of the story the idea is central for Rust and his antagonist, the so-called "Man with Green Ears." Whereas for Errol Childress the flat circle girds a twisted personal mythology, for Rust, the circularity of time seems more like a *problem*, a discouraging and pessimistic description of life and reality.

We can see this in the lengthiest description of circular time, which comes when Rust is interviewed by Detectives Gilbough and Papania in 2012. Rust says:

> Someone once told me that time is a flat circle. Everything we've ever done or will do, we're gonna do over and over and over again. And that little boy and that little girl, they're gonna be in that room again and again and again forever. ("The Secret Fate of All Life")

Rust, in this moment, seems almost paralyzed, philosophically speaking. Reggie Ledoux is the one who told him about the flat

True Detective and Philosophy: A Deeper Kind of Darkness, First Edition.
Edited by Jacob Graham and Tom Sparrow.
© 2018 John Wiley & Sons Ltd. Published 2018 by John Wiley & Sons Ltd.

circle, and at the time Rust quickly attributed the quote to Friedrich Nietzsche (1844–1900). Indeed, the "flat circle" is a reference to what some philosophers call "eternal recurrence" or "the eternal return of the same," and Nietzsche is the notion's most famous expositor.

How is it that here, in the interview with the detectives, Rust seems so paralyzed, so stuck, but by the end of the narrative he claims to have seen the "light"? To figure out what this "flat circle" means and how it fits into the story, we have to understand Rust's general philosophy and how it relates to Nietzsche, as well as to the work of Arthur Schopenhauer (1788–1860), a famous philosophical pessimist and important influence on Nietzsche.

Rust's Philosophy: Pessimism and the Escape from Time

The idea of the flat circle ultimately helps Rust to overcome his bleak interpretation of reality, although for a long time it anchors him in his dreary worldview. Thus the flat circle operates as both problem and solution for Rust. After his near-death experience, he interprets his old actions with a new sense of closure and hopefulness. But, to understand how the flat circle can at once trap Rust and set him free, we have to examine his philosophical pessimism, noting how it is not equivalent to nihilism—in spite of the fact that Rust sometimes comes off as nihilistic. Even Marty says, in "The Locked Room," "for a guy who sees no point in existence, you sure fret about it an awful lot."

A philosophical pessimist is likely to view knowledge and meaning as inherently flawed. They are also likely to doubt that existence can be good or happy, yet be likely to believe that existence is defined by fundamental suffering. The nihilist, by contrast, denies that anything has meaning or value. Life is neither good nor evil, neither happy nor sad, for the true nihilist.

Rust tells Marty all about his philosophical pessimism in the first episode of season one. He remarks that "we are creatures that should not exist by natural law" and he also says that all humankind should "walk hand in hand into extinction." These are classic pessimistic views: the first human, a supposedly conscious being, was an abomination or deviation from the course of nature (Rust says), and it would be better to have never been born at all, since no one asks or chooses to exist. Furthermore, in our existence we are guilty. In "Seeing Things," Rust speaks of the "incredible hubris" that is required to give birth to children, to "yank a soul out of nonexistence." When Rust asks Gilbough and Papania, "Why should I exist in history?" he exemplifies his commitment to the idea that he cannot justify why he should exist at all ("The Secret Fate of All Life"). Rust never chose to enter this situation where suffering reigns. Realizing this, he looks for an escape.

Indeed, for the philosophical pessimist, death is the only escape from life's miseries. And yet, the form of dying affects the pessimist's position on the matter. Schopenhauer, a well-known pessimist, suggests that many forms of suicide are unsatisfactory because they involve succumbing to one's will, rather than denying it. The denial of the will is the proper response to life, Schopenhauer claims, because it is the will that's responsible for all suffering. He claims in *The World as Will and Representation* that, if you're going to kill yourself, you should do something like starve yourself, since this is true self-denial.[1]

Maybe now we know what Rust means when he says that he lacks the proper "constitution for suicide" ("The Long Bright Dark"). He welcomes death several times throughout the series, and in "The Long Bright Dark" he praises a crucifix for symbolizing the idea of "allowing your own crucifixion." This would be an example of denying one's will in permitting another to kill you.[2] Christ, as God, could have prevented his own death—but elected not to do so. In spite of his atheism, Rust admires this. After visiting Miss Dolores in "After You've Gone," he says, "I sure hope that lady was wrong ... about death not being the end of it." All he means here is that he hopes that death really is the escape from life's miseries. That is, he hopes that his death is a solution, even though he cannot will suicide.

Nietzsche, too, is a philosophical pessimist, but he is not a proponent of nihilism. In fact, he condemns it. For example, in the *On the Genealogy of Morality*, he predicts that, if humanity does not alter its course, it will be forced to face total nihilism.[3] Nietzsche claims that people can create their own meaning and value in a world that seemingly offers nothing in terms of absolute, ideal meaning or significance. The same goes for Rust. To be a nihilist, he'd need to give up the idea that existence has a negative value. Not only this, but he'd have to drop all compassion altogether.[4] He obviously thinks, at least for a while, that existence is just something in which we suffer. But existence is *not nothing*. To be sure, Rust sometimes teeters on the edge of nihilism, as when he talks in "The Locked Room" of "meat puppets" and everyone's "dream about being a person." But the flat circle, if Rust really believes in it, is an idea that can help him ward off not only nihilism but also the pessimism in which the idea originates. It is Rust's talk of death as a solution, as escape, that demonstrates that he is in fact far from content with his philosophical pessimism. He wants a way out.

Does Rust Really Believe Time Is Circular?

We eventually find out that Rust is still working on the Yellow King case, so he cannot view his actions as totally pointless. Some meaning must still exist for him, otherwise he would not continue chasing a solution. But there's a problem: Why, in the 2012 interview with the detectives, does Rust come off so philosophically dejected? Is he just throwing the detectives for a loop when he describes, in one of the most famous scenes, the flat circle of time?

I don't think this is the case. Rust describes M-theory physics to the detectives, in apparent scientific support for what otherwise looks like a pretty mystical notion about reincarnation. But this isn't enough to prove that Rust really believes in the flat circle, which isn't in fact about reincarnation at all. The primary reason why we should take Rust seriously when he talks about the flat circle is a very straightforward one: he keeps bringing it up and, historically, the idea of circular time has been tied to—you guessed it—philosophical pessimism. Yet, in fact, circular time is supposed to be a prescription for *overcoming* pessimism, even if, until you can overcome it, the circle practically confines you to the pessimistic paradigm. Such is the case with Rust.

After his interview with the detectives, Rust mentions circular time twice more before the final showdown at the Carcosa maze. He isn't just trying to influence people. Rather, he keeps talking about the flat circle because he really believes in it, in a thoroughly pessimistic manner. He says things like "nothing is ever over" and he dismisses the idea that closure is ultimately attainable. His long speech about the "secret fate of all life," in the episode of the same name, is a description of the endless repetition of time and life and, somehow, death. But later it is the idea of the flat circle that helps Rust see this is a mistake.

For now, let's proceed on the assumption that Rust believes in circular time and isn't just using the idea for rhetorical effect. What exactly is it that Rust believes about time and circularity and how does this liberate him from pessimism?

What Does "Time is a Flat Circle" Not Mean?

At first it is hard for us to tell what Rust really means, especially when he brings up M-theory, a scientific theory that describes the nature of reality. If Rust believes this theory, then "time is a flat circle" is as literally true as the force of gravity in nature. A philosopher would call this a cosmological or metaphysical claim.

A metaphysical claim tries to describe the true nature of reality. Such a claim is even more basic and primary than the claim a physicist makes about reality, because a metaphysical claim purports to address the background reality that supports physics. You've likely heard of the most famous metaphysical idea of all: God. Rust isn't a fan of the idea of God, and I don't think it's likely he means "time is a flat circle" in a metaphysical sense.

Nor do I think that Rust likely means this cosmologically. A cosmology is a "science of the stars" or "heavens," and even though Rust mentions M-theory he isn't talking about it because he's interested in the scientific claims it involves. Rust doesn't care about theoretical physics. Rust likes one thing about M-theory. He likes that, if M-theory is accurate science, then our linear perspective of time is as relative as the hypothetical perspective of a point on a Cartesian coordinate system compared to our experience of three-dimensional space. In short, Rust likes the pessimistic existential implications that M-theory could offer, and M-theory pulls Rust in the opposite direction from his ultimate conversion experience.

Rust emphasizes that eternity looks down upon us as "flat." By this he means that our choices and our lives are, in the grand scheme of things, insignificant. This is another example of Rust's bleak philosophy, but this is more nihilistic than pessimistic. It's actually not a particularly useful idea for Rust, unlike the flat circle. So, even though M-theory and the flat circle resonate on certain levels, they aren't identical.

Maybe you still think that there is something literal about the flat circle. Perhaps you're thinking of the swirling, ominous vortex that hovers over Rust's head in the Carcosa maze. Rust does not actually see this vortex the way he sees Marty, however. At Carcosa he is face to face with an ecstatic vision representing his guiding idea— the circle. We know that Rust is prone to hallucinations from his undercover drug use, and, apart from his mental experience, there is presumably no "external" or "supernatural" vortex that you or I would have seen, were we present in the same room.

We have to try to view the eternal recurrence as Rust might experience it, rather than from a position in an audience. To fully understand what Rust's flat circle means, we have to strive to relate to him, which is to say, insofar as we are able to do so, endeavor to think and also *feel* the story from his position. If we take on Rust's view, and consult again the thought of Nietzsche, we can see that the flat circle is a philosophical tool, a thought experiment.

Nietzsche's Eternal Recurrence

Nietzsche, like Rust, meant for circular time to be a thought experiment rather than a scientific theory.[5] Nietzsche calls his theory "eternal recurrence," but, difference in name aside, there are numerous similarities between his theory and Rust's. The point of Nietzsche's idea is what's so useful for Rust, even though he suffers in his preoccupation with circularity, at least until the final episode, when he tells Marty he's ready to tie his circle off. Shortly after this, he "sees the light."

We should assume that Rust is familiar with Nietzsche, because the first time we hear about time and its circular flatness, in "The Secret Fate of All Life," Rust mentions Nietzsche by name. He points a gun at Reggie Ledoux, silencing him. We can assume that this means that Rust has not yet adopted for himself the idea of the flat circle, although he has already entered his "circle of violence and degradation." This is after his daughter dies, his marriage falls apart, and he begins undercover narcotics work in Texas, until he gets injured and is committed to a mental institution. This arc continues as Rust returns to police work in Louisiana and culminates in Rust's second hospitalization.

Presumably Rust identifies the circle when he returns to Alaska after leaving Louisiana in 2002. During this isolation, we can surmise that Rust had much time alone with his thoughts. For Nietzsche, the idea of the eternal recurrence needs to be conscious if it's going to be of any use to you, since the point is to view every decision differently. He writes:

> What if, some day or night a demon were to steal after you into your loneliest loneliness and say to you: "This life as you now live it and have lived it, you will have to live once more and innumerable times more." ... Would you not throw yourself down and gnash your teeth and curse the demon who spoke thus? Or have you once experienced a tremendous moment when you would have answered him: "You are a god and never have I heard anything more divine."[6]

The idea is that, if you truly endorse the actions that comprise your life, then to hear that you would relive your life forever would be a sort of heavenly experience. If you are not proud of your actions, wishing in retrospect that you had done otherwise, then this news would be equivalent to damnation, to pure horror. You could hear nothing worse than that you'd be forced to repeat your life over and over again. To avoid this, then, one must make great decisions. Rust isn't particularly proud of a lot of the decisions he has made since he entered his own personal circle. But, at the same time, it's apparent that he experiences a "tremendous moment" in the final episode.

Nietzsche thinks that, if you can live by the idea of eternal recurrence, then you can ultimately affirm life in spite of your myriad dissatisfactions. To live your life like this is, for Nietzsche, to love fate itself, *amor fati*.[7] This is how you overcome both pessimism and nihilism, and also the circularity of insignificant action and choice: precisely by assuming circularity, here rendered differently as fate. It is in this way that you achieve greatness. The idea of the flat circle, then, is supposed to change your life. It's not at all supposed to be a prison that establishes the insignificance or unhappiness of your human condition. That's only one side of it, the side you fall on if you look down on your choices. Is it not here that Errol Childress falls?

Schopenhauer too talks of eternal recurrence, and his remarks are useful in evaluating Rust. For Schopenhauer, even if someone has not yet realized that "constant suffering is essential to all life," she can nevertheless desire "that the course of her life as she had hitherto experienced it should be of endless duration or of constant recurrence" and furthermore can even "willingly and gladly put up with all the hardships and miseries" of life.[8] This is exactly what Rust does as he devotes himself to the unsolved case, while his toleration of life's difficulty is not manifest until he nearly dies and thereby sees how valuable his work has been. This is the flat circle at work.

And yet, if you remember that Rust is a card-carrying pessimist, you should note that, for most of the first season, Rust does *not*, in any sense of the expression, *affirm* life or maintain that anything about himself or reality is great. However, in the final episode, "Form and Void," Rust, is ultimately able to overcome it by "seeing the light" that leads him to question all of his old "definitions." This encounter with greatness, this "tremendous moment," brings Rust to tears because he doesn't have to regret the course of his life—he can now *love* everything that has come to pass because he has seen, beyond his bleak, pessimistic worldview, the face of his daughter. Rust now loves fate.

In spite of his pessimism, it's precisely the thought of the eternal recurrence that preoccupies Rust until ultimately he transcends the worldview. He would never come to this redemption if not for his obsession over the Yellow King case—mediated in his actions.

Circular Time as a Solution that Replaces a Pessimistic Problem

The flat circle is really a thought experiment that Rust remains trapped within insofar as he remains a philosophical pessimist, at least up to the point of his near-death experience, where he "sees the light." The stormy, spinning vortex in the Carcosa maze is not only a hallucination for Rust but also a powerful visual symbol for the viewer—especially when we note that soon after this Rust nearly dies and encounters his dead daughter in a heavenly light. The stormy vortex represents Rust's troubled psychology, but it also represents the peaceful calm that follows. This is Rust's philosophical recovery. His sickness has been intellectual rather than physiological, and this is why the psych ward did him more harm than good.

The flat circle is a problem packaged with its own solution, albeit one requiring great courage. We have to assume that Rust's coming to the light is authentic because the eternal recurrence itself calls for this overcoming. Thinking of time circularly can render action pointless, but what the thought really invokes is a path to action that is profoundly meaningful. Indeed, Nietzsche hopes that it does not move you to horror, but joy. Before this joy is attainable, though, you face anxiety about your existence—and maybe this is why Rust sometimes sounds so nihilistic as he tries to cope. Here we might think of the philosopher Martin Heidegger (1889–1976), who claims in his famous *Being and Time* that anxiety about one's death should not be troubling or debilitating but, rather, should empower one to live meaningfully.[9] This is precisely where we find Rust in the final episode, with the knowledge and purpose he needs to live a meaningful existence. Nonetheless, this knowledge is the result of agony and pain, symbolically reflected in Rust's atheistic admiration of Christ. Rust goes right up to the edge of death in sacrificing himself—physically but also in his withdrawal from social life—in order to work toward justice.

After his near-death vision, Rust shows willingness and desire to affirm life, even the bad, when he awakes in the hospital in "Form and Void." Outside he tells Marty that the latter is interpreting the night sky wrong: he says that it isn't that there is more darkness than starry light but that, at one point in time, darkness is all there was. Can we imagine Rust saying this before he had some grasp of a reunion with his daughter?

In short, for Rust the flat circle isn't simply a "negative" idea, precisely because it brings him full circle to overcome his condition. Even though it seems like Rust may be mired in the thought of the flat circle, his obsession with the idea of being stuck in a circle forever keeps him on the Yellow King case, 10 years after the state police closed it. It's an idea that, at least for a while, keeps him rooted in his stark pessimism, but it's also the means to Rust's ultimate end: saving himself *from* himself, *from* his pessimism. In the end, Rust realizes that there is more to the truth than the starkness of suffering and despair—he escapes the flat circle by faithfully acknowledging the flat circle. The way Rust achieves this can be summed up in one word: sacrifice.

Notes

1. Arthur Schopenhauer, *The World as Will and Representation*, vol. 1, trans. E. F. J. Payne (New York: Dover, 1969), §69, 401.
2. Yet as one of my editors, Tom Sparrow, notes, isn't it also in a way the case that this permission is itself an act of the will?
3. Friedrich Nietzsche, "Third Essay," in *On the Genealogy of Morality*, trans. Carol Diethe, ed. Keith Ansell-Pearson (Cambridge: Cambridge University Press, 2007), §14, 89.
4. Rust's compassion is arguably one of the most central aspects of his character, in spite of his bleak pessimism.
5. Nietzsche briefly flirted with the fantasy that he could scientifically prove that time really is circular. He realized that this raised many paradoxes and that the important philosophical benefits of the idea required no empirical or scientific proof anyway.
6. Friedrich Nietzsche, *The Gay Science*, trans. Josefine Nauckhoff, ed. Bernard Williams (Cambridge: Cambridge University Press, 2001), §341, 194.
7. Ibid., §276, 157.
8. Schopenhauer, *The World as Will and Representation*, vol. 1, §54, 283–284.
9. For Heidegger, it is precisely the finite scope of one's life, rather than the idea of infinite repetition, that motivates you to existential purposefulness. See Martin Heidegger, *Being and Time*, trans. John Macquarrie and Edward Robinson (New York: Harper & Row, 1962), §40, 230–231.

Known Associates

Peter Brian Barry is the Finkbeiner Professor of Ethics at Saginaw Valley State University, USA. He is the author of *Evil and Moral Psychology* (2013) and *The Fiction of Evil* (2016), in addition to multiple articles in ethics and social and legal philosophy. Being incapable of guilt, he usually has a good time.

Chris Byron is a doctoral student and teaching assistant in philosophy at the University of Georgia, USA. He specializes in Marxism and political philosophy. He has published several book reviews and essays on human nature, and also an essay in *House of Cards and Philosophy* (Wiley Blackwell, 2016). He likes to pat himself on the back for sparing the world the sin of being a father.

Joshua Foa Dienstag is professor of political science and law at the University of California, Los Angeles, USA. He is the author of *Pessimism: Philosophy, Ethic, Spirit* (2006) and *Cinema, Democracy and Perfectionism* (2016). He has published many articles on the history of political thought, film, and democratic theory. An avowed pessimist, he believes time is more of a flat spiral and aspires to be bad at parties.

True Detective and Philosophy: A Deeper Kind of Darkness, First Edition.
Edited by Jacob Graham and Tom Sparrow.
© 2018 John Wiley & Sons Ltd. Published 2018 by John Wiley & Sons Ltd.

Paul A. DiGeorgio teaches philosophy at Duquesne University in Pittsburgh, USA, where he is also a doctoral candidate. He has published on Nietzsche and currently works on phenomenology, existentialism, and philosophy of religion. He admits that he cannot be sure that consciousness isn't a tragic misstep in evolution, but he worries that, if it is, then that doesn't bode well for graduate studies in philosophy.

Sarah K. Donovan is associate professor in the Department of Philosophy and Religious Studies at Wagner College, USA. Her teaching and research interests include community-based learning and feminist, social, moral, and Continental philosophy. While she admires existential heroes who find their way out of deep abysses, Cohle would still not be on her shortlist of people to call for advice.

Rick Elmore is assistant professor of philosophy at Appalachian State University, USA. He researches and teaches in twentieth-century French philosophy, critical theory, ethics, social political philosophy, environmental philosophy, and new realisms. He is the co-author of *The New Derrida* (forthcoming). His articles and essays have appeared in *Politics & Policy*, *Symploke*, *BioShock and Philosophy* (Wiley Blackwell, 2015), and *The Aesthetic Ground of Critical Theory* (2015), along with entries in the *Meillassoux Dictionary* (2014) and the *Nancy Dictionary* (2015), which is all to say, he's great at parties.

Jacob Graham is assistant professor of philosophy at Bridgewater College, USA. He's interested in ancient and modern philosophy, music, and baseball. He doesn't sport a gold grill, because that's no way to greet the world.

Lawrence J. Hatab is Louis I. Jaffe Professor of Philosophy and Eminent Scholar at Old Dominion University, USA. He has written six books, including *A Nietzschean Defense of Democracy* (1995), *Nietzsche's Life Sentence: Coming to Terms with Eternal Recurrence* (2005), and *Nietzsche's On the Genealogy of Morality* (2008). He is a recovering academic, has never solved a murder, and avoids pessimism with the maxim "Live every day as if it was someone else's life."

Alison Horbury lectures in the School of Culture & Communication at the University of Melbourne, Australia, and is the author of *Post-feminist Impasses in Popular Heroine Television: The Persephone Complex* (2015). Her research interests include Continental philosophy, post-feminisms, and popular screen cultures, and she is currently working on a project exploring the psychoanalytic ethics of popular and quality screen aesthetics. Like Ani's dad, she tends to think we should all spend less time in a state of resistance making problems for ourselves.

Luke Howie is in the School of Social Sciences at Monash University, Australia. He has published widely on the war on terror, the economic crisis, popular culture, and the amazing work of Slavoj Žižek. Luke had many dreams for his future when he was growing up, but he figures we all get the world we deserve.

Daniel P. Malloy is a biological puppet made of sentient meat, just like you. His programming has led to a life of teaching philosophy and writing about philosophy and popular culture. It's not a particularly raw deal. He's published chapters on *Dexter, Inception, The Big Lebowski*, Sherlock Holmes, and Hannibal Lecter, among others.

G. Randolph Mayes is a philosophy professor at California State University, Sacramento, USA. His main philosophical interests are naturalism and the nature of rational inquiry. Like Rust, he is bad at parties.

Christopher Mountenay is a creature who should not exist by natural law. He lives in Pittsburgh, Pennsylvania, with his wife, two cats, and lizard. He has a doctorate in philosophy, having written a dissertation on Nietzsche's early writings on pre-Platonic philosophy and Schopenhauer's pessimism. His programming also entails a deep love of weird fiction. He is currently looking to transition from academia to the less soul-destroying pursuit of paving the way for the awakening of the Great Old Ones. He can already smell the psychosphere …

Beau Mullen is a recent graduate of the Florida State College of Law, USA. He has published articles in aesthetics and political philosophy. He is convinced that sometimes your worst self is your best self.

Sandra Shapshay is associate professor of philosophy at Indiana University—Bloomington, USA, and directs the program in Political and Civic Engagement. Her research interests center on Schopenhauer, Kant, ethics, and aesthetics. Currently she is working on a book reconstructing Schopenhauer's ethical thought. In the 1990s, Shapshay once stunned her friends by giving Woody Harrelson lengthy directions to a bar in Soho, New York City, without realizing even for a nanosecond who he was. After *True Detective*, it is unlikely she would be able to give him directions without blushing.

Tom Sparrow is assistant professor of philosophy at Slippery Rock University, USA. His primary research is in Continental philosophy and phenomenology. He is, most recently, the author of *Plastic Bodies* (2015) and *The End of Phenomenology* (2014). At the risk of certain disappointment, he dreams of the day when the highways and byways of America will be lined with Vietnamese cafés.

Evan Thompson is professor of philosophy at the University of British Columbia, Canada, and a fellow of the Royal Society of Canada. He is the author of *Colour Vision: A Study in Cognitive Science and the Philosophy of Perception* (1995), *Mind in Life: Biology, Phenomenology, and the Sciences of Mind* (2007), and *Waking, Dreaming, Being: Self and Consciousness in Neuroscience, Meditation, and Philosophy* (2015) and a co-author of *The Embodied Mind: Cognitive Science and Human Experience* (1991). He has long wondered whether life is a kind of dream, whether the self is an illusion, and what happens to the dream of being a self when we die.

Daniel Tutt teaches philosophy at Marymount University, USA. He has published articles on Lacanian psychoanalysis, political philosophy, and theology in outlets such as *The Huffington Post*, the

International Journal of Žižek Studies, the *Journal of the Society for Contemporary Thought and the Islamicate World*, *Philosophy Now*, and *The Washington Post*. Like Cohle, he reads philosophy to help conquer his symptom.

Chuck Ward teaches philosophy at Millersville University, USA. His scholarship is usually focused on the philosophy of science (specifically biology) and on the philosophy of mind and neuroscience. Lately he is spending more time in dark streets and dark bars such as the Black Rose. Mostly this is through literature or TV shows, but occasionally in the flesh. Despite some tendency to turn a philosophical lens toward the darker side of human beings, he is an optimist about the power of philosophy to make things more bearable. So he won't say this is his least favorite life. It may, in fact, be his most favorite.

Andrew M. Winters earned his Ph.D. in philosophy from the University of South Florida, USA. He is instructor in philosophy at Slippery Rock University, USA. While awaiting the time when he'll no longer exist, he conducts research in the metaphysics of science.

Index

True Detective and Philosophy: A Deeper Kind of Darkness, First Edition.
Edited by Jacob Graham and Tom Sparrow.
© 2018 John Wiley & Sons Ltd. Published 2018 by John Wiley & Sons Ltd.

Printed and bound by CPI Group (UK) Ltd, Croydon, CR0 4YY

29/01/2024

08228714-0001